the gift basket design book

second edition

Everything You Need to Know to Create Beautiful,
Professional-Looking Gift Baskets for All Occasions

shirley george frazier

gpp

Guilford, Connecticut

To John, Genesis, Mom, Cassandra,
and Aunt Shirley, the loves of my life.

To all of the designers, store owners, and product
manufacturers who have helped to make gift baskets
a worldwide phenomenon.

Text design: Nancy Freeborn
Photo credits: All photos are courtesy of the author.

ISSN 1548-1557
ISBN 978-0-7627-4436-7

Manufactured in China
Second Edition/First Printing

Contents

Introduction

Why I Began Making Gift Baskets

Mix a cup of fun and inspiration with the love of creating something beautiful with your own hands, and what do you get? A gorgeous, timeless gift that everyone will remember and treasure for a lifetime. When I began searching for a career that provided satisfaction, gift baskets never entered the picture. I trained to be a secretary, but I soon found working for someone else to be boring. In ten years I worked for ten different companies. So I began searching for a profession that would challenge my creativity.

My great-grandmother Mary Smith grew her own strawberries in Virginia and shipped them to Manhattan during the early 1900s. In the 1940s a great-aunt made fudge, and my mother was her delivery person. My father was co-owner of a chemical company in the 1970s. Their pursuits sealed my fate as an entrepreneur, but you don't have to find creativity in your family to be bitten by the gift basket bug. What most designers share is a love of making something beautiful with their hands. If you possess this trait, you'll love gift baskets.

My mother enrolled me in sewing classes when I was ten. I knitted and crocheted in my teen years, and I've always loved arts and crafts. You couldn't pry me away from making jack-o'-lanterns at camp. Were you the same way? That's part of what gift basket designers have in common.

In the 1980s computers were becoming a hot commodity. I wanted to start a word-processing service, but I quickly gave up that idea and replaced it with one to open an intimate-apparel boutique. I'm fascinated by retailing and have worked in both small and large stores. Since ladies love lingerie, it seemed to be a good match. Then my husband, John, made a gift for a coworker. He took a small bottle of liqueur and paired it with a shot glass, gluing rocks to the bottom. He covered it in plastic wrap and added a small bow on top. The recipient loved it. John's thoughtfulness is what led me to a career making gift baskets.

If you're interested in making one single gift basket, that's fine. But if you want to keep your hands constantly submerged in the shred and cellophane, you can do that, too. There's always a birthday or celebration where a gift basket is welcomed. We also make baskets to apologize for an error, help folks get back on their feet, and bring comfort in times of grief.

My design ideas were somewhat strange at the beginning. For instance, I thought a gift for people who were afraid of dental work would be popular. Instead of using a basket, I'd use a giant, hollow enamel tooth cut in half with a hinge in the back to hold it together so that gift items could be placed between the two parts. Another idea was to calm individuals afraid of airplane travel. A miniature suitcase would hold items (cards, dice, puzzle books, and so on) that kept people busy en route.

Choosing containers rather than baskets is part of the creativity. I've always been captivated by unique containers, because it sets the gift apart from traditional baskets. That's what drew people to my designs. A dish drainer housed the new-home gift, a child's wagon welcomed the new baby, and a miniature rocking chair symbolized retirement, all holding gifts and snacks for the receiver.

Baskets are more beautiful today than when I started designing. Some are made with wire, and others contain sophisticated trim or hardware. It can be difficult to choose a vessel because each one is more gorgeous than the next.

Gift baskets are a joy to make, and anything goes, as long as you can piece it together. Being creative is fun, but sometimes a design is so large and challenging that it takes hours to make. Some of us will sit back and marvel over it when completed. Others will critique it to death, fixing this and that to the point that we take the whole thing apart and start all over again. That's how passionately designers feel about gift baskets, and I'm excited to share the passion with you.

Before we get started, let me introduce you to some words you'll find throughout this book. Many are used interchangeably, and I want to ensure that you understand each meaning.

- *Baskets, containers,* and *vessels* represent the same thing. All three words refer to the foundation that holds the contents you've chosen for your designs.
- *Cavity* refers to the inside opening of a basket or container. It's the area filled with packing paper or tissue-covered floral foam.
- *Cellophane, cello, plastic film,* and *closure material* describe the product that encloses the basket, protecting the contents until the recipient removes it to enjoy the contents.
- *Contents, product,* and *item* refer to anything that is placed within a basket, container, or vessel. This includes, but is not limited to, snacks, gifts, shred, and enhancements.
- *Enhancements* and *embellishments* have similar meanings and describe the "flora and fauna" added to your baskets.
- *Floral foam, Sahara,* and *brick* share the same meaning.

- A *gift basket designer* is also known as a *pro* or *professional*.
- *Gifts* are items that are inedible. Examples include stationery, coasters, and cookbooks.
- The *receiver* or *recipient* is the person for whom the gift is being made.
- *Snacks* and *foods* are used interchangeably, referring to anything that people can eat or drink.

Popcorn, chocolates, and coffee are part of this category.

Whether you make gift baskets for fun or want to take your skill further and start a business, this book will provide you with many ideas to create beautiful gift baskets for everyone in your life.

PART 01

Design Basics

01 Humble Beginnings, Fabulous Future

Creating a Work of Art for Every Occasion

Joy and amazement occur every time I teach a gift basket design class. The group of aspiring beginners enters the room, empties the contents of a large bag onto the work table, and stares at the basket and products in front of them, all in disorder as though it were a broken puzzle. The work begins. You can hear a pin drop as the budding designers concentrate on how to fill their baskets with chocolates, chips, bottled water, and other goods. Then there's lots of noise as twenty pairs of hands crunch and crush paper, filling the baskets' cavities simultaneously. Someone snaps a skewer into three pieces. Fingers tuck shred neatly between products that stand tall like soldiers. Leaves and brightly colored flowers find a place within the vibrant designs. Clear cellophane bags rattle as they surround and encase each creation. Everyone is talking and laughing during the final step of topping the new design with a dazzling, handmade bow.

The puzzle is complete. One by one, the new designers gasp and admire the masterpieces before them. What emerges from controlled chaos is a group of individuals who've completed their first lesson in professional gift basket design. They smile broadly and are eager to learn more. But first, they notice something unexpected. Each person was given the same products, yet every basket looks different. How could something that started out the same end up looking so dissimilar? The answer lies in two words: *individual creativity.*

Every designer, whether beginner or expert, has a vision of how to make a gift basket. The construction always changes, even when making multiples of the same design. That's what makes this bundle so fascinating and such a joy to make or receive. And there's always something new and exciting to unleash your creative genius.

A Quick History Lesson

I thought gift baskets were a fairly new phenomenon when I started making them in 1989. Magazines on the topic had yet to be published, and videos were nonexistent. All those who were making baskets kept their design skills a closely guarded secret.

Little did I know that the gift basket dates back to at least 1913, when it was first mentioned in *Woman's Home Companion,* a magazine that's reminiscent of today's supermarket journals. The article "Baskets for the New Baby" included photographs of baskets and suggested baby gift items—bibs, brushes, combs, soaps, and powders. There was no mention of wrapping everything in cellophane, but the idea was there, and uncovering it was monumental for me.

House of Wembdon, a New York–based toiletries manufacturer, advertised its gift basket sets in the *New Yorker* in 1937. Its baskets ranged in price from $1.50 to $5.00, and the price of a jumbo-sized $15.00 basket must have seemed like a king's ransom during the Depression.

A 1943 article in the magazine *House Beautiful* proclaimed gift baskets as "something to give the rich." The Christmas baskets were themed for cocktail parties, potluck dinners, and Asian cuisine and ranged in price from $7.00 to $11.50. Some of the contents, such as mixed nuts and popcorn, are still popular today, while anchovy fillets and turkey a la king have fallen out of favor.

Gift baskets were a favorite of *Sunset,* a California lifestyles magazine, which frequently showed designs on its pages. One 1956 article titled "How to Pack a Gift Basket" featured a step-by-step guide on combining fresh fruits with canned and jarred foods. It also showed how to add cellophane and a bow.

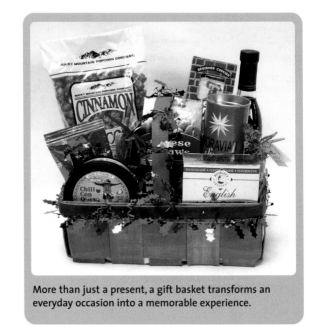

More than just a present, a gift basket transforms an everyday occasion into a memorable experience.

I gathered this history in the summer of 2000 while searching through the New York Public Library archives. Photos, advertisements, and articles appeared in magazines that were so old they nearly disintegrated when I touched them. Gift baskets have stood the test of time, through strong and weak economies. And the myth about gift baskets being a new industry faded almost as fast as it began.

Why Gift Baskets Are Popular

If you give someone a picture frame, it's a gift. But when you present the same person with a gift basket consisting of the frame surrounded by candles, bath salts, a music CD, body powder, and lotion, you give a mood-altering experience. You wait to see the expression on the recipient's face—the pleasure and excitement all at once. That's what separates presenting a gift basket from the mere act of giving a gift.

Don't be surprised if the receiver doesn't open your gift basket—ever. For some, the creation is too exquisite to disturb. This has happened to me numerous times. I'll fill an order and deliver it if it's not too far from my workshop. The recipients are overjoyed and ask me to come in and sit for a while. I wonder if I have a trustworthy face, or is it that I've presented them with a treasure and they want to share this joyful moment? Sometimes I can stay a while, and other times I must rush off to another delivery.

If I stay, it's not uncommon for the recipients to place the gift on a table with other decorative items and state that it will sit there forever. For some, the memory of receiving the basket is more significant than the contents. What's really important is that the receivers love what you've created. You may find yourself telling them what's inside and warning that if the food products aren't eaten within a specified period, they'll no longer be edible. Other times you might consider placing a label on the bottom stating this fact as a reminder.

I love it when a person enjoys the basket's contents, and I also consider it an honor to make a design that becomes a collector's item. Some designers don't feel the same way. They want the person to open and eat or use the contents. But should you make the recipient part with such beauty? After you've designed and delivered the basket, it's okay to let go of your "baby" and move on to other designs.

People never tire of receiving gift baskets. The vessel is different, the contents change, the embellishments depict the occasion or season, and there's always a surprise inside. No other gift promises such

Many basket recipients don't open their gifts—ever.

delight. That's why you're ready to make your own, and I'll show you how.

You'll find making gift baskets to be fun and rewarding. Perhaps you are looking for general knowledge about this skill, or maybe you know how to make baskets but want to elevate your expertise. This book will help you do both. First you'll learn about the supplies and tools needed in your workspace. Then we'll get into design techniques that the pros have mastered. I can't wait to get you started.

Basic Supplies

Most of us are mesmerized when we see gift baskets in boutiques, specialty shops, and department stores. Their composition reveals a well-thought-out selection of foods and gifts surrounded by clear or colorful packaging. What we don't see is the construction hidden underneath.

Gift-basket-building techniques aren't always simple, but designers use the same products in creative ways to make each design unique and different. Gift baskets are created with a collection of items, some of which you're familiar with and others that you've probably seen in a craft store but never knew how to use. After combining everything together to form a gift basket, you'll step back and wonder why you waited so long to create your first masterpiece.

The Essentials

Here's a look at the items you'll consider buying to make your first basket. You'll find sources for all the items mentioned here listed in the Resource section at the end of this book.

An Attractive Basket

Select a basket of any color and size that's made with a sturdy wood frame. Make sure that the basket's weave is smooth and unbroken on all sides as well as on the bottom and handle. When placed on the floor, a well-made basket sits flat and doesn't wobble. Your first basket, whether square, round, oval, or rectangular, should include a handle.

A basket with a depth of 4 to 5 inches is a good size for practice. It will give you enough space to create a design that includes five or six items. Also, it's best not to select a plastic basket such as the type used by a child for Easter egg hunting. A tightly woven basket made from wood is the vessel of choice to create a design that looks like it was made by a professional.

TIP: Add color to an unpainted wooden basket by spraying it with nontoxic paint in an aerosol can. Apply the paint outdoors, if possible, or in a well-ventilated space. Use gloves and a pair of goggles to reduce hazards and cleanup.

Newspaper or Packing Paper

Single sheets of crumpled paper are used to fill the basket's inside opening. Newspaper is a popular item that many designers choose, but some are against it because the ink can transfer from paper to hands. An alternative is to use packing paper. This plain paper, usually packaged in boxes to protect mail-order items, is tan, beige, or brown in color. It is rigid and more voluminous than newspaper, so less is needed to fill the inside basket.

Commercial packaging stores and wholesale gift basket suppliers (listed in the Resource section) sell packing paper on a roll, but to save money you can start saving the packing paper that comes in packages you receive from mail-order companies. Old wrapping paper is another alternative. Styrofoam peanuts can also be used, but they are less desirable because they can move inside the basket, making the foods and gifts shift unexpectedly.

Shred

Every basket contains shred. It's a material most often made from wood or paper and molded into various

Start with a sturdy wooden basket of any color or size.

Crumpled paper is used to fill a basket's interior.

Shred provides a colorful cushion between the basket and its contents.

forms. That's why shred has many names—parchment, excelsior, Mylar, tissue, and sizzle (also known as crinkle).

Some shreds are coarse and stiff, while others are soft and spongy. All of them provide a colorful cushion on top of the newspaper or packing paper, in between the basket and snacks. Your choice of shred depends on what you like and what looks best in the design.

Snacks and Foods

The basket's contents are the main attraction—that's what makes people melt with delight. The most popular snack items are:

- Chocolates
- Cookies
- Popcorn
- Potato chips
- Pretzels
- Nuts
- Crackers
- Cheese
- Beef sausage
- Jams and jellies
- Coffee, cocoa, and tea

There are many other products to select, but these items are chosen most often because each can be opened and eaten immediately, giving the recipient instant gratification. Another reason for this group's popularity is that you can design many themes with these same products. All of them are great for birthdays, thank-you gifts, housewarmings, and other

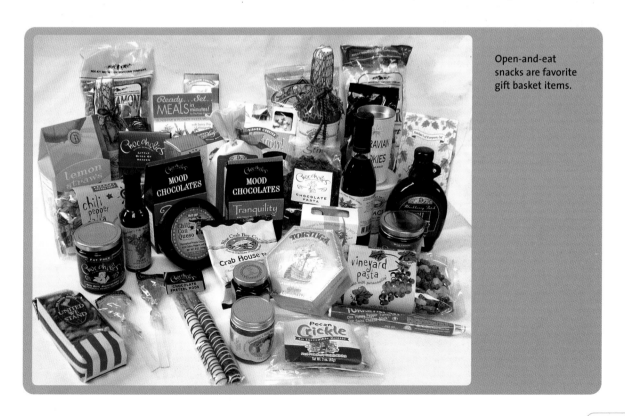

Open-and-eat snacks are favorite gift basket items.

everyday events. Each product is prepackaged and ready for purchasing at local stores, which is why open-and-eat snacks are the best items to fill your baskets.

FACT: Some cheeses need refrigeration, but others can be stored in a cabinet or container. Cheeses made with preservatives that allow them to be kept at room temperature are just as delicious as the refrigerated kind.

Silk Flowers and Picks

You don't have to be a botanist to select flowers that create a soft and pretty appearance inside the basket. Flowers are the long-stemmed beauties that are added to the back and sides of the basket, while picks are short (with approximately 2-inch stems) and placed in the front.

Daisies, gyp (gypsophila), pansies, and violets are four great choices, and there are others. Look at the different varieties at your local craft store. Determine which flowers and picks will enhance your designs without overwhelming the foods and gifts.

Cellophane or Basket Bag

A basket and its contents are enclosed in a thin plastic film that keeps the design in place until it's opened. Cellophane is available on a wide roll, usually 20, 30, or 40 inches in width and 25, 50, or 100 feet long. Basket bags are precut to fit many basket sizes and shapes. Cellophane and bags are made in a clear film or decorated with flowers, fruit, hearts, dots, phrases, and other prints.

Another way to close your gift baskets is to use shrink wrap, which is described later in this chapter.

Use flowers and picks to add interest.

Enclose your baskets in plain or printed cellophane or bags.

Add bows for a gorgeous enhancement.

Premade and Handmade Bows

A pretty bow tied around the closing at the top (also known as the neck) of a basket complements the attractive design. Premade bows are simple to make and available in many sizes, colors, and styles. They are purchased flat, and when you pull the two slim ribbons that accompany the wider ribbon, you create a gorgeous bow in less than ten seconds.

Designers often choose to make a bow "from scratch" to enhance their baskets. This type of bow is known as "handmade." It's created using ribbon available in craft stores on 25, 50, and 100 foot rolls. There are videos and tabletop machines available at retail stores and on the Internet (sources are listed in the Resource section at the end of this book) to teach you how to make your own bows.

Look at all the available ribbon and bow styles at craft stores before making your choice. One basket may look best with a solid-colored bow tie, while another will sparkle when topped with a large multi-colored puff bow.

Scissors and Other Supplies

You will be cutting many items such as cellophane and tissue paper, so a good pair of shears is essential to creating great designs.

Your scissors must be sharp, and that means investing in a sharpening tool or outside sharpener (craft or knife store retailer). This will ensure quick cutting the first time, as well as preventing any injuries that may result in medical attention. Some designers also use small, all-purpose cutters or electric scissors when cutting cellophane for orders in excess of a hundred baskets.

Sharp cutting tools are critical to the basket maker.

Transparent tape secures cellophane around the basket.

A sharp knife is handy if you plan to cut floral foam to place inside of your baskets, as you'll learn in chapter 3. As with scissors, one clean cut into the foam will keep your design time to a minimum.

Wire cutters are perfect for flowers, picks, and other enhancements with overly long stems. Such stems should be cut before they're included in a basket. Scissors are ruined by running them over the thick wire, so wire cutters are the best solution. Craft and gift basket suppliers sell these tools. Read the packaging to determine which wire cutters to buy before making your choice.

Keep a roll of transparent tape handy. It's needed to secure cellophane around the basket, and you'll use it for other tasks as well.

More Helpful Products

The items from the previous groups form the basis for designing your gorgeous gift baskets. But there's more to review before you start. If you want to include heavy bottles such as cider and syrups in your baskets, there are special supplies to consider buying for extra support. They will help you anchor, secure, and add interest to your designs. Here are some additions to the basic supplies.

Gifts

Not all baskets are made solely with snacks. There are many fun and thoughtful keepsake items that are perfect for baskets. These include:

- Gift books
- Bath and body products
- Mugs
- Stationery and writing instruments
- Key chains
- Cookbooks
- Candles
- Utensils
- Picture frames
- Napkins
- Plush toys
- Plant seeds
- Gardening tools

Gifts within baskets will be treasured long after the occasion has passed.

- Baby items
- Drinking glasses
- Antistress toys

Gifts are very popular, so consider adding these items to your gift baskets as a memento that will be around when the snacks are gone.

Floral Foam

Floral foam is a product that helps to stabilize snacks and gifts inside the basket. It is gray and shaped like a brick but is very lightweight. Also known as Sahara, it's a dry material that's gritty to the touch. It is used most often by florists to support silk flower arrangements.

Do not confuse floral foam with Oasis, which is usually green in color. Although both products are rectangular in shape, Oasis acts as a sponge to hold water when soaked and is used to preserve fresh flowers and plants.

TIP: Use a long knife to carve the floral foam so that it fits snugly just below the basket's rim. Trim the foam sparingly so as not to cut too much at one time. You'll see this technique in chapter 3.

Tissue Paper

If you use floral foam, it's best to cover it with tissue paper before placing it inside the basket. The tissue keeps the foam from transferring onto the receiver's hands or clothes. Tissue also acts as a shield between the foam and the snacks and gifts placed on top of it. Any tissue paper color is acceptable because it will be hidden from view once the basket is completed.

Another use for tissue paper is as a concealer between the packing paper and basket. This is needed when a basket contains an open weave, allowing the

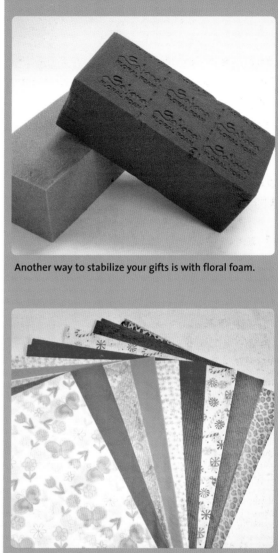

Another way to stabilize your gifts is with floral foam.

Use tissue paper to cover floral foam.

packing paper to be exposed. An example is shown in chapter 3.

Embellishments

Why add only flowers to baskets when there are so many decorative items to choose from? Stroll through the aisles of a local craft store and you'll see more alternatives that add a creative touch.

What all embellishments have in common is that each is supported by a long, slim stem. Among the decorative touches to look for are butterflies, frosted balloons, onion grass, and picks (mentioned earlier under "Silk Flowers and Picks"). You'll see how to add embellishments in chapter 5.

Any number of embellishments can add sparkle to your creations.

Bamboo Skewers

These long, thin polished pieces of wood aren't just for the barbecue. Skewers are paired with floral foam to make snacks and gifts magically stand straight. The top of a skewer is attached with transparent tape to the front, back, or side of a snack or gift item. The bottom of the same skewer is inserted into the foam. The snack or gift will stand upright inside the basket with help from the skewer. You'll see this simple technique in chapter 4.

Skewers allow your gift items to stand upright.

Double-Coated Tape

Why would anyone need tape that's sticky on both sides? This is what designers use to hide skewers from sight. When a skewer is secured with transparent tape onto a snack or gift, it must be masked so that no one sees the anchoring technique.

Place double-coated tape on top of the transparent tape. Then press a pinch of shred atop the double-coated tape, and the skewer vanishes, leaving everyone to wonder "How do you do that?" This will also be shown in chapter 4.

Double-sided tape is another designers' secret.

Shrink Wrap

Cellophane and basket bags provide what's called a soft wrap around a gift basket. But if you prefer a tight, crystal-clear appearance, shrink wrap will provide it. Shrink wrap is the closing material that most retail stores select. A machine dispenses the wrap, and a heat gun shrinks and seals the wrap around the design.

Craft stores also sell shrink wrap on rolls and in shell formats (shrink wrap bags with rounded top edges), eliminating the need for the shrink wrap machine. Both are priced for the budget-conscious designer. With each product, you'll need to use a heat gun to shrink the film around the basket.

In lieu of a professional heat gun, some new designers shrink the wrap with a hair dryer. You may find that your home dryer's settings are better for hair than for shrink wrap, but this is the time to experiment. If the hair dryer doesn't work to your specifications, a low-cost heat gun is a worthwhile investment. Chapter 6 will show you shrink-wrapping techniques.

Hot Glue Gun

Enhancements such as flowers, ribbons, and bows sometimes need extra support to stay in place. Glue sticks are inserted into a hot glue gun, which turns the hard glue into a liquid. The softened glue that is pressed from the gun creates a bond between the embellishment and the chosen surface.

Hot glue is used between cellophane and ribbon to create a rippled effect on the outside of the basket, or it can keep flowers securely in place on the cellophane. Use hot glue safely and responsibly. Once applied, it is difficult to remove.

Glue Dots

Here's a product you can use instead of or in addition to a hot glue gun. Glue dots are preformed sticky circles that bond two or more things together. These puffy, neutral-colored dots are available in varied strengths of stickiness (tacky, very tacky, and highly tacky). They're dispensed on a roll and ready to join anything within the basket. Unlike hot glue, these dots are easily removed from any surface.

Curling Ribbon

This thin, wavy ribbon wrapped on 5-inch spools is most often added around the neck of a basket where the main bow holds the outside wrapping (cellophane, basket bag, or shrink wrap) in place.

Once the curling ribbon is tied and knotted, the ends hang downward. These ends can be curled with scissors or a ribbon cutter to create a curly haired effect around the basket.

TIP: Tie several curling ribbon colors around the basket's neck to add extra pizzazz to the design.

These additional items will become as important to you as the basic gift-basket-making products. One of the best things about making gift baskets is that very little is thrown away. For example, old cellophane can be used to fill an empty basket opening instead of or in addition to newspaper or packing paper. Embellishments that tear or break apart are easily added in a different area of the basket (shown in chapter 12). There are other ways to recycle old and worn-out supplies that I'll share with you throughout this book. First, however, you need to learn where to find gift basket supplies.

Where to Find Supplies

Gift basket snacks, gifts, and enhancements line the aisles of many stores that you routinely visit.

A heat gun and shrink wrap will give you a tighter package.

A hot glue gun and glue sticks bond enhancements to the outer wrap.

Glue dots bond items together within the basket.

Curling ribbon closes and embellishes the outer wrap.

Craft stores such as Michaels, Ben Franklin, and A. C. Moore sell many of the supplies that complete your gift basket designs, including vast selections of baskets, shred, flowers, bows, curling ribbon, tissue paper, and other tools. Search each aisle thoroughly to view all your options. Inspect the baskets stacked on tiered shelves and in bins. Familiarize yourself with the flowers, pore over the ribbon selections, and see all the available shreds. If you've never combed through a craft store, you'll find this first outing to be a fun and enlightening experience.

Before buying new baskets, look around your own home for vessels that you've collected in years past. Some attics and basements harbor elegant woven creations that will now be put to good use. Your search may also reveal other stored items to enhance your designs.

TIP: Live in a rural area? Use pinecones found in your backyard instead of buying them from a craft store. Once the basket is filled, pinecones are used as an enhancement along the basket's inside rim. Microwave the cones individually for one to two minutes to rid them of microscopic organisms, or heat them in an oven at 400 degrees for five to six minutes. Spray the cones with a nontoxic silver-, copper-, or gold-colored paint.

Another place to find goods is at flea markets, swap meets, and garage sales. Check each basket's construction before making a purchase. You'll find many items at these places to use as gifts and enhancements. Proceed slowly and be careful not to overpurchase. Select only the items you truly believe will go into your baskets.

Supermarkets, gourmet shops, and candy stores sell delicious snacks and goods that will fill baskets. Supermarkets also sell bamboo skewers in the gadgets aisle. Edibles are found in a variety of stores, including pharmacies, cosmetics stores, and discount chains.

Office supply stores (Staples and its counterparts) sell transparent and double-coated tapes, and they occasionally place mugs and post-Christmas snacks on clearance tables. If you belong to a warehouse club such as Costco, Sam's, or BJ's, these stores also sell many gift-basket-friendly items.

Don't overlook the linen chains. Years ago my daughter worked at one such store. She brought home soups, vinegars, and cookies packaged in cute boxes, bottles, and jars, all less than $1 each. The soups were packaged in jars with flowered fabric tied with cord around the lid. These specialty items are perfect for gift baskets, and the price is often lower than wholesale.

Professional florists purchase silk flowers and supplies from floral wholesalers, which are located in cities nationwide. Although conflicting stories are told, some of these outlets will allow the general public to buy. Professional designers are card-carrying members of these companies who do not pay sales tax because they resell products to the public. If you are able to purchase supplies, you will pay sales tax, but the savings are enormous and so is the selection of baskets, silk flowers, picks, ribbons, balloons, and more.

One drawback is that some products are sold by the dozen, but if the cost is low, it may be worth buying. Consider how many gift basket designs those eleven other items can be used in. Check your Yellow Pages under "Floral Suppliers" or "Floral Wholesalers" to see if there's one in your area. Call and ask if general consumers are able to buy merchandise. If you are given the green light, it's a trip that's worth your time.

TIP: When visiting a floral wholesaler, think and act like a professional. Don't announce to fellow shoppers that you're a crafty person and that this is your first visit. Professional florists will not appreciate knowing that you're invading their territory. Inspect the aisles of merchandise as though you're in a craft store. Make your selections, pay for the supplies, and leave with the satisfaction that you've found great items to create many designs.

Also visit dollar stores and off-price discounters, which sell many types of gifts and goodies. Look for pretty tote bags and mugs, which you'll learn to design in chapter 11. Don't overlook candles, fragrances, and frames—three more products that dollar stores stock until a new batch arrives, just in time to make more gift baskets.

03 Preparing the Inner Basket

Two Simple Ways to Fill Your Container

Before designers assemble their creations, they must prepare the inner basket. This involves filling the basket or container with a base material to elevate the contents so that foods and gifts can be seen above the basket's rim. There are two options for filling a basket: (1) newspaper or packing paper or (2) floral foam and tissue paper.

The supplies you'll need are:

- One medium-sized basket with handle, any shape. The basket should have no partitions on the inside.
- Three ounces of shred, any type. Three handfuls is equivalent to three ounces.
- Approximately 2 feet of packing paper or four full sheets of newspaper.
- One floral foam brick and one sheet of tissue paper, any color.

Select a basket with the same width from the top to bottom. Baskets that are wider on top need more products to look full. Your basket should also be flat on the bottom so that it doesn't wobble when filled. Take a minute and place the basket on the floor. If it sits flat, you've chosen a good vessel. If not, select a sturdier one.

TIP: Choose a workspace floor of wood, marble, or other nonfabric surface. Shred has a tendency to migrate downward and is easily removed by sweeping or vacuuming an uncovered floor.

Select a medium-sized basket with a handle...

...but not one with inner partitions.

It's easiest to work with a basket that's the same width from top to bottom...

...because a basket that's wider on top needs more products.

Option 1: Newspaper or Packing Paper

Set your basket on a sturdy table or horizontal work-space. If the basket is made with a tight weave (the slats are against each other), then you can proceed to fill it with paper. If the basket contains an open weave, however, it must be lined with tissue before the paper is added. This will keep the newspaper or packing paper from being seen through the slats, which detracts from the presentation.

Crumple one sheet of newspaper within your hands, and insert the wadded paper into the basket. For packing paper, use a piece approximately 25 inches in length. Continue to crumple additional paper, and insert it until the inside of the basket is filled. Use your fist to press the paper firmly downward into the basket. Do not be gentle; you are building a tight foundation so that the contents will stay in place and above the rim rather than sink down into the basket.

Continue to add crumpled paper on the inside until there is approximately 1 inch of empty space between the top of the paper and the basket's rim. Make sure the paper is tightly packed. Have additional paper available in case you need more.

Add an even amount of shred on top of the paper. The shred should be even with or slightly above the basket's rim. When finished, you should not be able to see any paper on the inside. Shred that falls over the rim is acceptable. It's a material that cannot be tamed, so let it hang.

1. Line an open-weave basket with tissue before filling it.

2. The tissue should prevent newspaper or packing paper from peeking through.

3. Add crumpled paper to the basket.

(continued)

4. Press the paper down firmly with your fist.

5. Continue adding paper to about 1 inch from the basket's rim.

6. Topping the basket with shred hides the paper from view.

7. Shred has a will of its own!

Option 2: Floral Foam and Tissue Paper

Floral foam is approximately 9 inches long, 4 inches wide, and 3 inches deep. In most (but not all) cases, it will have to be cut or trimmed to fit the basket's cavity.

Place the foam on top of the basket to determine how much should be cut. This is best done by estimation, though you can mark the foam using a pen or pencil for support. Put the foam on the table and begin cutting it into shape. Be careful not to cut too much at one time. Return the foam to the basket. If it fits, you're ready to cover it with tissue paper. If not, continue trimming until it sits comfortably inside the basket.

TIP: For large or oversized baskets, fasten two foam bricks together using U-shaped pins. Place the two bricks together where joining will occur, and insert a pin's ends into each brick. Put one pin in the middle, or place two pins about 1 inch apart, including a pin on the opposite (bottom) side if needed.

Because of the basket's depth, the foam might be positioned well below the rim. This is remedied by adding paper to the basket's bottom as described in Option 1. The difference is that here you'll add a small amount of paper to raise the foam, rather than filling the entire basket with paper. Start with two crumpled pieces. Press each into place. Insert the foam to test its height. When the foam is even with the rim, you're ready to proceed.

Before the carved foam is inserted, it must be covered with tissue paper. Products will sit on top and should not do so on the exposed foam, which is gritty and unattractive. Even if you use a brick in a color other than gray (bricks are made in various colors), it should still be covered.

1. Floral foam makes an excellent basket-filling alternative.

2. You'll probably need to trim the foam to fit your vessel.

3. Cut the foam a little at a time. You can always trim more later.

(continued)

4. Keep trimming until the foam sits comfortably inside the basket.

5. U-shaped pins let you join two foam bricks.

6. Insert one end of a pin into each brick.

7. You can use more than one pin if needed.

8. Adjust the foam's height by adding wadded paper at the bottom of the basket.

9. Fold a piece of tissue in half.

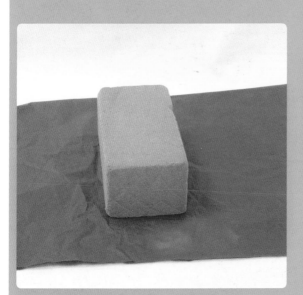

10. Place the foam brick facedown on the tissue.

11. Enclose the brick in paper, closing with transparent tape.

(continued)

12. Wrap one end of the brick as you would a Christmas present.

13. Trim excess tissue from the other end, then finish the same way.

14. Your covered foam brick should fit snugly in the basket.

15. Fill any empty spaces with shred. You're ready to add snacks and gifts.

Fold the tissue paper in half. Place the brick in the middle of the tissue, with the top of the foam facing downward. (You can tell which side to put facedown based on how you trimmed the brick to sit inside the basket.) Wrap the tissue around the foam, and close it using one piece of transparent tape. Trim any excess tissue from the opposite end. Then close and tape it. Place the covered foam within the basket. The fit should be snug. Add shred to the basket in the gaps between it and the foam. Keep the top of the foam empty for now. It will soon hold snack and gift items.

Which Method Should You Choose?

Gift basket designers use both methods to fill the inner basket, according to their preference, skill level, and the types of products to be included. The foam-and-skewer method accommodates a basket with a heavy beverage bottle. A paper bottom works well for children's baskets, because skewers may prove dangerous to the recipient. Try both options to familiarize yourself with the techniques. Like the professionals, you may find yourself using one method for a certain design and a different method for the next.

Basket Filler Dos and Don'ts

Over time you might encounter other filler options. Here are a few tips:

- *Do* substitute old cellophane for newspaper and packing paper. Cellophane is just as easy to crumple and this is an excellent way to recycle cellophane that's worn or dusty.
- *Don't* use Styrofoam peanuts as a basket filler. This product can be an unstable and undependable foundation material. Some professionals have mastered their designs using peanuts (as you'll learn in chapter 13), and you may do so in the future. For now, however, working with paper or foam and skewers is best.

Basic Building Techniques

Proper Placement of Snacks and Gifts

If you've ever tried to make a gift basket without knowing how to make foods stand upright, the contents were probably tilted at a forty-five-degree angle. This chapter will teach you two methods to solve this problem by properly anchoring your products. The first method uses the paper-filled basket and glue dots; the second combines the floral-foam-filled basket with bamboo skewers. These techniques correspond with chapter 3, where you learned how to fill your basket with either paper or floral foam.

For Option 1, you'll need:

- Basket filled with packing paper
- Snacks and/or gifts
- Glue dots

or for Option 2, assemble:

- Basket filled with tissue-covered floral foam
- Skewers
- Transparent tape
- Double-sided tape
- Snacks and/or gifts

The basket you select should be sized in proportion to the number of items to be included. For example, a medium-sized basket, approximately 11 inches in diameter, will hold seven to eight items without looking sparse when complete.

Option 1: Paper Method

This technique is for the basket that contains tightly packed paper topped with shred.

Group all the contents together on your tabletop or workspace. To design your basket, taller items will be placed in the back, graduating to the shortest items in front. This basket will include popcorn, two types of cookies, crackers, a turkey roll, cheese, jam, and water. These products are commonly used in basket themes such as birthday, thank-you, good luck, and congratulations. You can modify each arrangement by selecting ribbon and tissue colors,

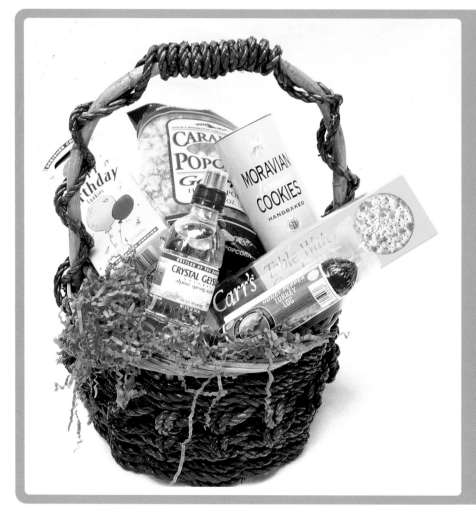

Unless you know how to make products stand tall and look attractive, your baskets will probably look like this!

1. Assemble your gifts according to height.

2. To create a basket using the paper method, begin by making an opening in the shred with your hand.

3. Fill the opening with your tallest product—in this case, popcorn.

4. Tidy up each package as you insert it.

(continued)

5. Adding a glue dot between popcorn and handle . . .

6. . . . will help hold the product upright.

7. Continue adding products one by one, the taller ones in back . . .

8. . . . and the shorter ones in front.

embellishments, and product labels that denote the occasion. For example, a product labeled HAPPY BIRTHDAY would be added to a birthday basket, as shown for this design.

Each product will enter the basket at a specified insertion point within the shred and on top of the paper. The popcorn is the tallest item and will be added first. Use your hand to make an opening (hole) within the shred. This exposes the paper so that the popcorn will sit on top. Next, add the popcorn into the opening. Lightly press the popcorn down onto the paper, and lift the shred up and around the popcorn. About ¼ inch of shred will sit around each item after it is inserted. The popcorn now sits firmly in place. Look at the item and fix the top of the package to remove any crumpled edges. This type of bottom-to-top inspection is required for each product.

TIP: Not all products have to face forward. Some items can face sideways or backward. It's your design. Experiment!

Contents often need support to stand tall or up against each other. For example, the popcorn may tilt toward the front. This is a temporary situation; it will stand straight as other products are added. If your basket's handle is positioned from front to back, you can place a glue dot between the back of the popcorn's packaging and the inside of the handle. Once done, the popcorn should stand tall on its own until the receiver removes the bag.

Continue adding each product, working with taller items in back and shorter ones in front. Glue dots can be placed between products that need extra support.

Keep All Labels Visible

Once your products are positioned, you need to assess whether the placement is really working. For instance, shorter items shouldn't be buried so deep within the shred that the receiver (and you) cannot see their names. An example of this is the jar of jam (shown below).

Rather than hiding it, elevate the jar by first removing the item, then adding a small amount of extra paper on top of the packed paper. Press the new paper down firmly. Put the product back in place, and add shred around it. The design is correct if you can see all or part of the product's name.

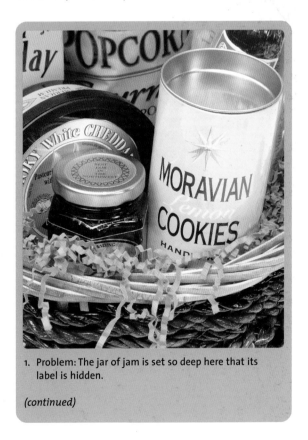

1. Problem: The jar of jam is set so deep here that its label is hidden.

(continued)

2. Solution: Remove the jam and add a bit more wadded paper, pressing down firmly.

3. Return the jar to the basket, touching up with shred.

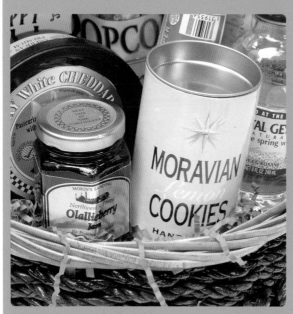

4. Now the jam is clearly visible.

5. Step back and inspect your finished basket. Can you see all or part of each product's name?

Option 2: Skewer Method

Gift basket designers in all stages—beginners, intermediates, and experts—use the skewering method. This is especially true when securing a large bottled beverage or something similarly heavy. For this design, we will use the basket with tissue-covered floral foam.

Select the products that will be added to the basket, and place them on the tabletop along with five skewers. Each product will be placed within the basket using the same method as for the nonskewered design: tall in back, short in front. The first item, popcorn, will not need a skewer, because the opening between the basket and foam is large enough to fit the bag. Remove some of the shred within the opening, and then carefully push the popcorn down into place.

The next step is to add a skewer to the cookie box. Break a skewer into three pieces, setting two of them aside. Determine where the skewer will be taped onto the box. In this example, the skewer will be taped in back. Using your thumb, hold one-third of the skewer against the box. The rest hangs below. Cut a piece of transparent tape long enough to cover the skewer resting against the box. Place the tape directly on top of the skewer.

Cut a piece of double-coated tape to exactly the same size as the transparent tape. Put the double-coated tape directly on top of the transparent tape (on the box). Now grab a fingerful of shred, and press it against the double-coated tape. This technique masks the skewer and will blend into the shred to be added later. Hold the cookies, placing your thumb or index finger atop the covered skewer. Gently bring the box down onto the foam, piercing the tissue with the skewer as it is inserted. To keep the cookies from twisting, secure the box with a piece of transparent tape and place it evenly between the box and the foam.

Continue to add products within the basket using the skewering technique. As with the popcorn, you may find that some products fit snugly in the openings between the foam and basket. When completed, add shred to hide the tissue-covered foam. Look closely, and fill in all gaps. Inspect your design to ensure that the tissue and skewers are masked.

This basket looks exactly like the packed-paper basket. Because of your masking techniques, you'd never know that skewers were added. Your gorgeous design is ready for enhancements.

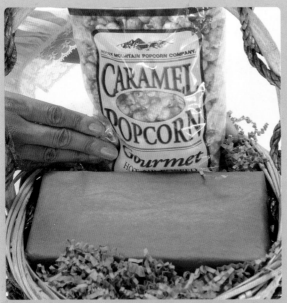

1. To assemble a basket using the skewer method, begin by placing the tallest product between basket and foam.

2. Break a skewer into three evenly sized pieces.

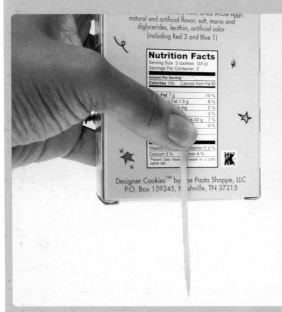

3. Hold one-third of the skewer piece against the cookie box using your thumb. Tape the skewer into place.

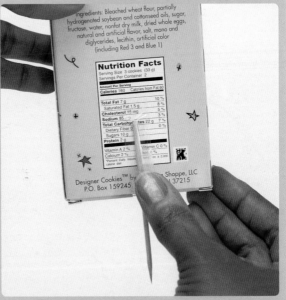

4. Cover the transparent tape with double-sided tape.

5. Press the shred into the two-sided tape so that the skewer is hidden from view.

6. Gently insert the skewer into your foam brick.

7. To keep the cookies firmly in place, add a piece of tape between box and foam.

8. Complete the assembly by adding shred as needed. Your basket is ready for embellishments.

05 Finishing Touches

Choosing Enhancements That Bring Your Design Together

There are many beautiful products out there that add dazzle to baskets and pull the theme together. If you are making a birthday basket, you might choose frosted balloons, star spray, and a festive pick. For a new baby, pink or blue embellishments are the best choices.

Other ideas are:

- Onion grass
- Star spray
- Flags
- Birds
- Flowers
- Ivy and other greenery
- Many other products that you'll find at craft shops

There's also twisted tamboo grass, which is known by the nickname "ting-ting." It's a product made from thin strands of wood that are straight at the bottom and curled at the top. Each strand is heavily coated with a sparkly substance in gold, silver, blue, red, and other colors. Ting-ting is tall, so you'll need to shorten the stems using wire cutters or breaking it apart with your hands before adding it. Be careful if you're breaking the stems between your fingers, because these artificial fibers are splintery and can become embedded in your skin.

Pull together your basket's theme with a multitude of embellishments.

Ting-ting is popular with basket makers.

Shorten ting-ting's stems with wire cutters or with your hands.

If your basket is packed with wadded paper, use shears to create a hole for embellishments.

You'll need wire cutters to shorten some enhancements.

Use scissors to curl bits of star spray for an interesting effect.

You can also wrap star spray around your finger to create curls.

Insert star spray into the hole you created with your scissors.

Medium-height enhancements can be added to a basket's sides.

Diminutive picks look great in front.

The three enhancements in this basket—star spray, medium pick, and short pick—look terrific together.

You may encounter difficulty adding enhancements to a paper-packed basket due to the stems' inability to pierce the paper. Use your scissors or another sharp object to make a hole in the paper. If needed, temporarily remove the shred in the area to access the paper. Then insert your enhancement. Deepen the hole if necessary and repeat the process.

If your enhancement towers over the tallest part of the basket, shorten the stem with wire cutters. This star spray embellishment is purchased tall and straight. Add character to it by carefully curling the grassy pieces with the open blade of your scissors. Curl the wired stars around your finger, and then gently pull the stars up for elevation. Now you can add the star spray to the design within the hole created by your scissors.

Inserting enhancements is easier in a floral-foam-filled basket. As with skewers, stems pierce through the foam, allowing the enhancement to stand upright. Repositioning embellishments in foam is a simple process: Just pull the pick up and out and reinsert it wherever it looks more attractive.

Place tall enhancements, such as ting-ting and star spray, in the back and sides of your design. Medium-size picks look great on the side, and short picks are best placed in front. Try not to overwhelm

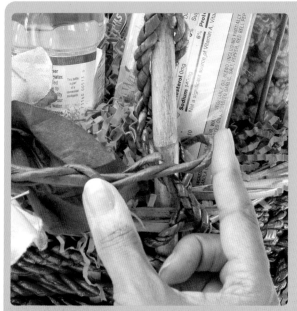

Wrap the wire ends of swag around the basket's handles.

Position the swag around the rim.

Grapevines can be tucked or pinned into place.

Complete your basket's look by adjusting the embellishments. Fan out the wired parts.

your design with assorted embellishments. Too many items can make your basket look busy and over-shadow the wonderful snacks and gifts. This basket (see page 42) includes three enhancements and looks terrific.

TIP: Ting-ting is another embellishment that serves as a short pick. Break the long stems, leaving 2 inches on the bottom. Add the shortened ting-ting to the front of your design.

Ivy can be wound from end to end around the basket's handle. Swags and grapes, two more popular embellishments, are often positioned around the basket's rim. Swags contain wired ends, which are bent and secured around the handle directly where the basket and handle intersect. Grapevines are soft and should be tucked between the inside basket and packed paper. If your basket contains floral foam, secure the grapevine's ends with U-shaped pins. The prongs are inserted into the foam, holding the vines in place.

Picks with wired parts, such as the medium pick of glittered berries and leaves added on the left side, contain branches that can be fanned out between, around, and above the contents. Now the basket is ready to be wrapped.

Your basket is ready to be wrapped.

TIP: Try not to be overly critical when placing enhancements. Most new designers believe that their work is not up to par with other baskets. We've all felt that way, and it's just a matter of time before you begin to see the beauty in your work. Finish the design, add the picks, and walk away for thirty minutes. Then return and inspect the basket. It probably looks better than when you left the room.

06

Closing the Basket

Proper Wrapping for a Professional Look

There was a time when you had only one choice of materials to wrap your baskets. Now there are three: (1) cellophane closure, (2) basket bag closure, and (3) shrink wrap closure. All three methods produce fine results.

Each designer selects a basket-closing method after weighing the following factors:

- *Budget*. What supplies can you afford to purchase at present?
- *Ease of use*. You'll need dexterity to work with a shrink wrap machine and heat gun.
- *Expertise*. Extensive experience equals more money invested for supplies.

Most new designers learn how to close their baskets using cellophane because it's the easiest and most readily available product at a low price. Basket bags have grown in popularity and are considered easier to use than cello. However, it can be difficult to find bags when you begin designing.

Shrink wrap is the most costly investment, requiring a shrink wrap roll or shells, shrink-wrapping machine, and heat gun. These products can cost $300 and up but can be found at lower prices through discounters. There's also a way to shrink your wrap without a machine, which I'll explain later.

All three closing techniques are widely accepted. Simply decide on a product to close your baskets and get started. Over time you will either grow comfortable with that particular method and stick with it or decide to try others.

For this final basket-making step, you'll need:

- Cellophane *or* basket bag *or* shrink wrap roll or shell
- Heat gun or hair dryer (if using shrink wrap)
- Transparent tape
- Curling ribbon
- Bow
- Embellishment (optional)

Let's take a closer look at the many ways you can wrap your baskets.

Cellophane Closure

Cellophane rolls are made from plastic and can be purchased clear or printed. The most common cellophane roll is 30 inches wide by 100 inches long. This size is adequate for most baskets. However, cellophane rolls are also available 20 and 40 inches wide, which accommodate small and extra-large baskets, respectively.

To begin closing a basket with cellophane, roll the cellophane onto the table. Make sure that you roll it out in the underneath position, not overhand. This will ensure that the right side of the cello faces outward on your design.

Sit the basket on top of the rolled-out cellophane. Bring the front end up from the table. Extend it toward the ceiling, above the highest point of the basket. This end should cover the basket's front plus extend above the basket by about 10 inches. Increase the amount of cello to satisfy this requirement. Bring the roll of cello up the back in the same manner as the front side. Cut the cellophane, and set the roll aside.

Cellophane is a great basket-closing choice for beginners and is available printed or clear.

Basket bags are growing in popularity and are easy to use.

Shrink wrapping is a little more costly but creates the most professional-looking baskets.

1. To wrap your basket in cellophane, begin by rolling cello onto your work surface.

2. Unrolling from beneath ensures that the right side of the cello will face outward.

3. Place your basket on the cello and extend the material up around the front.

4. Bring the cello roll up around the back of the basket as well.

(continued)

5. Cut the cellophane about 10 inches above the basket's highest point.

6. Be sure there's an even amount of cello on the basket's top and sides.

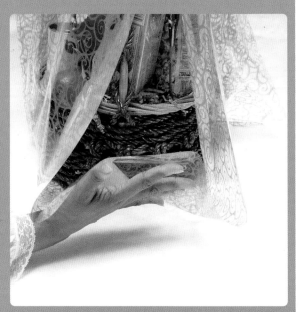

7. Bring the right sides of the cello together at the top and hold.

8. At the bottom, lift the cello up parallel with the basket's side. The cello is now roughly W-shaped.

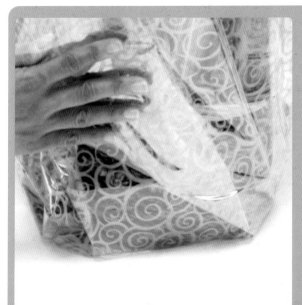

9. Fold the cello behind your fingers toward the front.

10. Now fold the remaining cello toward the back.

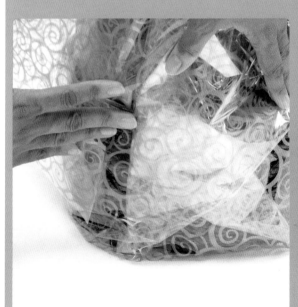

11. The cello is crisscrossed, resembling a triangle.

12. Secure the cello with a piece of transparent tape.

(continued)

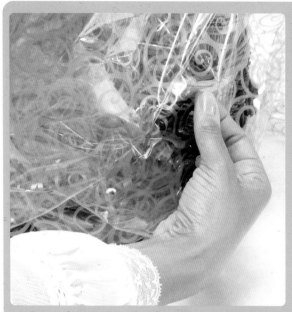

13. Repeat the process on the other side.

14. After taping, the cello should completely cover the basket.

15. Next gather the cello atop the basket into one hand.

16. With your other hand pull the cello up to tighten.

17. Position the bow to face the front of the basket.

18. Tie the two ends of ribbon into a knot in back.

19. Use transparent tape to fix any gaps in the cello.

20. To fix uneven cello above the bow, gather it between your fingers.

(continued)

Before closing the cellophane around the basket, measure it to ensure that the cello is even on the top and sides of the basket. Then return to holding both long pieces of cellophane at the top (around the basket's front and back).

With the front of the design facing you, bring the right side's edges together at the top and hold in place with your left hand. Working with your right hand, bring the cello lying flat on the table (the piece that connects the front to the back) up and parallel with the side of the basket. The cello's shape on the side now resembles a W or two Vs. In other words, one V of cello is in front of your wrist, and another V of cello is in back of your fingertips.

Fold the cello behind your fingertips toward the front. Then fold the remaining cello (formerly in front of your wrist) toward the back. The cello should resemble a triangle. Let go of the cellophane above the design (in your left hand), and secure the triangle-shaped cello with transparent tape. If needed, place a second piece of transparent tape 1 inch above the first piece. You'll need a second taping if the cellophane comes apart when your hands are removed. Repeat this process on the opposite side. Make sure that the last piece of folded cellophane points toward the back of the basket. This will give your design a polished, professional look.

Next, gather the cellophane atop the basket into one hand. With the other hand, pull the cellophane upward from end to end (front and back) to give the plastic film a clear appearance around the basket. Pick up the bow and position it to face the front of the

21. Cut the cello into a fan shape.

22. Voilà! Your gift is ready for giving.

basket, where your hands are gathered around the cellophane. Bring the curling ribbon strings around on each side of the cello (around either side of your hand) toward the back, and tie tightly into a knot. If desired, add more curling ribbon around the neck, and curl the long ends with scissors. You can also use a ribbon shredder to cut the ends into curly shreds (an example is shown with the basket bag; see page 55).

Fix any cellophane gaps that appear around the bottom of the basket by placing transparent tape on a gap, then pulling down and taping underneath. Do this wherever gaps appear. Finally, fix uneven cello above the bow by gathering the cello between your index fingers and thumbs. Cut the cello in a fan shape. Your basket is now ready for presentation.

Basket Bag Closure

Using a basket bag to close a design is said to be quicker and easier than using cellophane. For that reason alone, some designers prefer it. The bag is fused on three sides with an open end on top for easy basket insertion. The trick is selecting the right size bag for your basket.

A bag measuring 32 inches in height by 18 inches in width is a standard size that encases most medium-sized baskets. Measure your basket to determine the correct size bag. The chosen bag for your design should be 2 to 3 inches wider than the basket and at least 6 inches taller. This will give you just enough wiggle room to achieve a proper fit.

Starting at the top (open end), gather the bag together on both sides until you reach the (fused)

1. Many designers consider basket bags easier to use than cellophane.

2. To use a bag, begin gathering the material together from the top until you reach the bottom.

3. Use your fingers to spread the bag open on your work surface.

(continued)

4. Place the basket in the bag.

5. Carefully draw the bag upward until the basket is fully enclosed.

6. Now gather the bag at the top.

7. Smooth the bag by pulling upward.

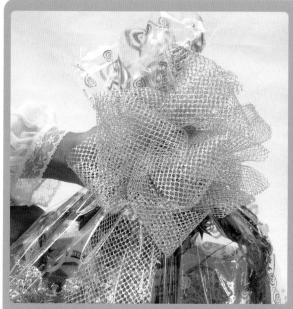

8. Tie the bow into place.

9. If you like, embellish with extra ribbon.

10. Here, a ribbon shredder is used to curl the ribbon.

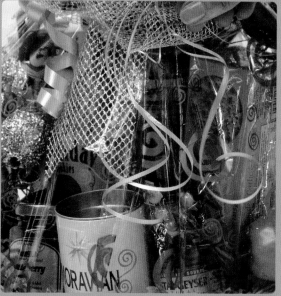

11. A pair of scissors will also give you this curly effect.

(continued)

bottom. Set the bag on the table, and place your index fingers and thumbs inside to open it widely. Set the basket inside the bag, then gently pull the bag up and over the basket. Be careful not to displace any of the basket's contents as you lift the bag upward. Once the bag has completely surrounded the basket, gather the bag together at the top. This is the same technique you used to close the cellophane wrapping.

Pull the bag upward to smooth the film around the design. When you're satisfied, add the bow around the neck and tie it into place. Add extra curling ribbon around the neck, and curl it with scissors or a ribbon shredder.

Choose one of the two methods shown on page 57 to smooth any bottom gaps:

TIP: Cellophane can still be pulled upward for a clear appearance, even after tying the bow and curling ribbon around it. This is important if the cellophane seems to be loose around the design. To check your bag for looseness, tug the cellophane at the top. Any additional looseness can be remedied by taping the cellophane down and under the basket.

• *The single-fold method:* Fold the bag back (in one fold) to the side, and tape it into place. Fold the excess underneath the basket and tape. Use tape to eliminate any leftover gaps. Finally, pull the tape downward, and secure.

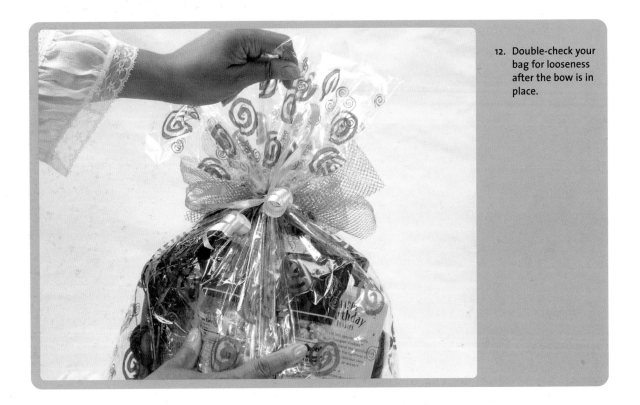

12. Double-check your bag for looseness after the bow is in place.

- *The multifold method:* Fold the bag in ½-inch folds toward the back of the basket until the bag is parallel with the side. Fold the excess bag underneath the basket, and tape into place using transparent tape. A small piece of tape might be needed on the side of the bag to secure the folds. Use tape to eliminate additional gaps around the bottom edges.

Your bagged basket is complete.

The single-fold method:

1. To narrow any gaps in the bottom, you can fold the bag to the side and apply tape.

2. Then tape any excess bag material beneath the basket. Pull the tape downward and secure.

The multifold method:

1. Another way to narrow any gaps is to fold the bag material toward the back of the basket in small folds.

2. Fold the excess beneath the basket and secure with tape.

Your design is complete. The bagged basket is ready for delivery.

Shrink Wrap Closure

Photographs in chapter 2 introduced you to the dynamic duo—the shrink wrap machine and heat gun. You also learned, however, that these aren't the only tools that will allow you to shrink-wrap your gift baskets. Craft stores also sell shrink wrap shells, which are bags with rounded top corners. And you can find shrink wrap on rolls that resemble cellophane but are clearly marked for use with a heat gun.

Shrink wrap machines are chosen by professionals who've decided to wrap most or all of their designs with this material. You can also add a shrink-wrapped look to your baskets at a fraction of the cost by purchasing a roll or shell. Here's how to use both.

Shrink Wrap Roll

Open the roll onto the table much as you would cellophane. Place your finished basket on top of the shrink, bringing the material evenly around the front and back of the basket. Add 10 inches above the tallest point in the basket. Cut the shrink wrap and set the roll aside. Remove the basket from atop the shrink wrap. Cut a long piece of curling ribbon (about arm's length), and place it to the side.

Upon closer inspection, you'll notice that the shrink wrap is doubled. One long side is a center seam, while the other side is unfused (open). Open the shrink wrap, undoubling it to become one large piece. Place the basket in the middle of the open wrap, and bring the shrink wrap evenly around the basket. Hold the shrink in one hand, and pull it upward toward the ceiling to give the wrapping a smooth appearance around the basket's bottom. Remove your hand while tying the curling ribbon around the gathered shrink wrap to keep it in place.

Place your heat gun or hair dryer on the highest setting, and begin shrinking the film on the bottom. Turn the basket by hand, using even strokes on the front, sides, and back. Don't keep the heat gun in one place too long—you'll risk tearing the film to expose a hole in the shrink wrap.

Gradually move upward to shrink the wrap, working steadily to make the wrap as tight as possible. Shrink wrap from a roll doesn't tighten as much as a shell, but it presents a good appearance when you're on a budget. Avoid shrinking the wrap above the curling ribbon. Before finishing, review your work and fix any unshrunk areas. Add a bow on top, and trim the shrink wrap above the curling ribbon. Your design is complete.

TIP: Take your time working with shrink wrap. The first few times you use a heat gun, you may end up with an uneven appearance or torn shrink around the basket. This is normal and will happen less often as you continue to practice with these materials.

1. Open a roll of shrink wrap much as you would cellophane.

2. Enclose the basket in shrink wrap, extending it about 10 inches over the top.

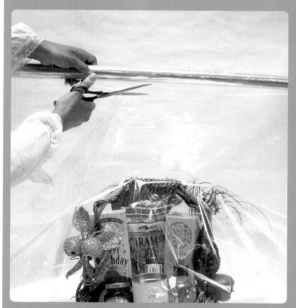

3. Cut the wrap. Remove the basket from the wrap and set it aside.

4. A close examination will reveal that shrink wrap is actually doubled.

(continued)

5. Open your piece of shrink wrap, place the basket atop it once again, and bring the wrap evenly up around it.

6. Pull upward to smooth the shrink wrap.

7. Tie a ribbon around the gathered shrink wrap.

8. Use a heat gun or hair dryer to shrink the film. Start from the bottom, and continue up the basket with even strokes.

9. Strive to make the wrap as tight as possible.

10. Put the finishing touches on your basket by adding a bow.

11. Trim the top.

12. Your gift is complete.

Shrink Wrap Shell

A shell contains a fused top with rounded corners and an open bottom. Open the bag using your fingers, and bring the open shell downward around the basket. Pick up the basket, and fold the excess shell underneath. Place two short pieces of transparent tape onto the opposite direction of the fold (across the shell) to close the excess neatly under the basket, and set the basket onto the table. There's no need to completely seal the shell with tape because the heat gun will seal the wrap.

TIP: Purchase a shell that's as close as possible to the size of your basket. This will ensure that there's no excess shrink material, which leaves an unsightly appearance.

2. Fold any excess shell material beneath the basket. Secure with tape.

3. Set the basket on your work surface for shrinking.

4. Carefully work your heat gun around the basket, beginning at the bottom.

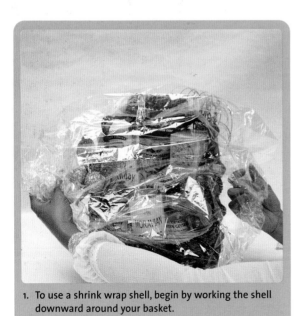

1. To use a shrink wrap shell, begin by working the shell downward around your basket.

5. Work your way upward.

6. Hold the extra wrap outward on each side and shrink until tight.

7. Use shears or a skewer to punch a hole in the shrink wrap for a bow.

8. Tie the bow into place.

(continued)

Begin shrinking the shell with your heat gun, starting on the bottom. Gradually work upward, saving the wide sides for last. Hold the extra wrap on one side outward with your hand, and shrink this area gradually until it's tight. Repeat on the opposite side. Inspect your work, and shrink the wrap on the underside of the basket before turning off the heat gun.

Use your scissors or the sharp end of a bamboo skewer to punch a small hole in the front and back of the shrink wrap where a bow will be placed. Carefully thread the bow's curling ribbon through the hole, and tie it into place. You can also add a self-stick bow, which does not require a hole in the shrink wrap. Self-stick bows, which are also sold in craft stores, contain a peel-off paper that reveals a sticky substance. Simply peel off the paper, and press it onto the shrink wrap.

Your shrink-wrapped gift basket is complete.

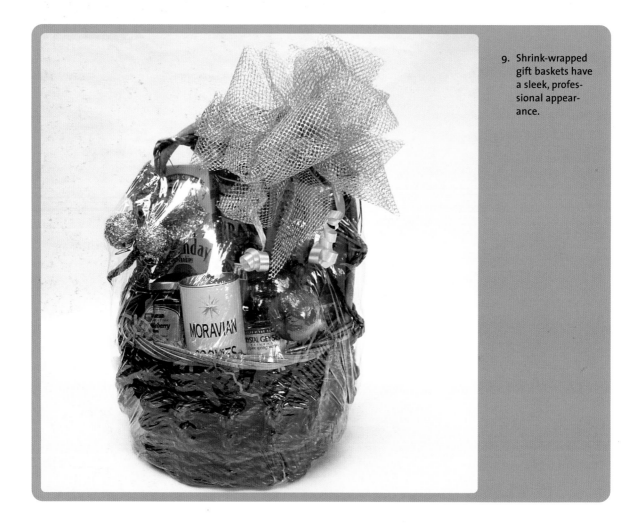

9. Shrink-wrapped gift baskets have a sleek, professional appearance.

One Last Look at Finishing Touches

Designers often add embellishments to the top of a design to add color and extend the height. You can achieve the same look by inserting star spray or balloons into the top of your cellophane or basket bag. Watch the stem of the star spray as it is inserted so that it does not puncture a product's packaging when lowered.

Holes in your shrink wrap caused by excessive heat can be masked by adding an embellishment. Trim the wired stem, if necessary, before insertion. Then bring the enhancement into the hole. Fan out any leaves on your pick. Add glue dots between the leaves and shrink wrap for added support. Note that the berry pick and leaves shown below hide any wrapping errors.

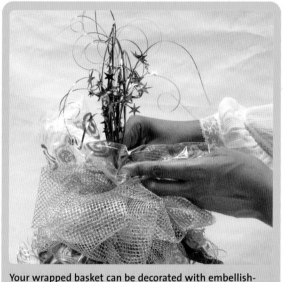

Your wrapped basket can be decorated with embellishments to add height . . .

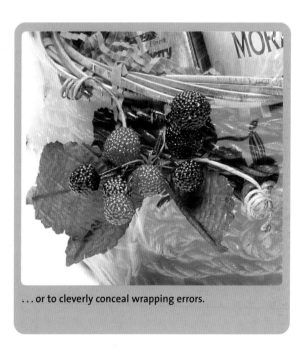

. . . or to cleverly conceal wrapping errors.

PART 02

Baskets for Different Occasions

07

Popular Occasions

Making Memorable Everyday Baskets

Each day, gift baskets are made and presented to people all over the world. The five designs shown in this chapter represent the most popular reasons for giving, as proven by statistics gathered from designers worldwide. You'll also find yourself making these baskets often.

Happy Birthday

There is no occasion more popular for gift basket giving than a birthday celebration. The basis for a terrific birthday basket is to know what types of snacks and gifts the recipient prefers. Does he like to cook? Then mixes and utensils create a satisfying gift. Does she love snacks with various flavors? Then that's what you choose. Also consider incorporating the person's favorite colors and gifts.

This birthday basket highlights blue, red, and orange colors. It's created using a medium-size royal blue–colored basket. The handle is attached on the sides, but the basket could just as easily have been designed with the handle stationed front to back. Blue tissue that coordinates with the basket's color lines the inner area, and it's topped with packing paper and sky blue–colored shred. If the recipient prefers a color other than blue, it's easy to change the basket and match it with coordinating shred. Added to this birthday basket are cranberry-orange cheese straws, amaretto-flavored cake, chocolate truffles, chocolate mint sticks, a canister containing mixed nuts, seasoned pretzels, a birthday-music CD, and coffee.

The Happy Birthday basket.

Choose birthday-themed gifts and snacks as well as products selected especially for the recipient.

Placing products at angles adds interest and appeal.

Floral enhancements need not be similar on both sides.

No tape or glue dots are needed in this design because the addition of greenery and short picks helps to stabilize the foods and gifts, making the items snug and secure. One branch of floral leaves in back on the right is taller than the other enhancements. It adds interest to the design and does not need symmetry on the opposite side, although you may add it within your own design for balance. That's part of the fun of making gift baskets. The design is created in a manner that looks best to *you*.

A box of chocolate truffles, added in front, sits at an angle to enhance this design's elegance. The birthday CD is also angled, and the words HAPPY BIRTHDAY printed at the top of the jewel case highlight the theme. It's simple to remove the CD to present this basket for a different occasion or replace it with a CD that refers to a different event. If the CD is positioned in the back or another area where the birthday phrase isn't visible, a placard similar to the one in the Congratulations basket, which announces the theme, could be added instead (see page 73).

In chapter 4 you learned that some gifts are best positioned facing backward. The chocolate mint sticks are an example of this. They're tucked in back, surrounded by foliage. Their blue packaging complements the basket, shred, and CD.

Birthday baskets can be filled with snacks and gifts or might reflect the wishes and desires of a

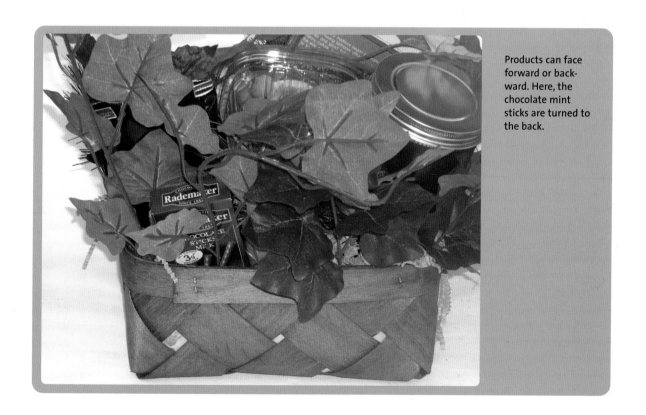

Products can face forward or backward. Here, the chocolate mint sticks are turned to the back.

person who seeks to start a new hobby in the coming months. For example, if the person expresses interest in scrapbooking, this basket might include any of the following: paper cutter, frames, ribbons, an archival-safe album, stickers, embellishments, adhesives, and templates. An alternative container for a scrapbooking birthday basket is a canvas tote with a scrapbook slogan embroidered on the outside. You'll see how to use different types of containers in chapters 10 and 11.

A person who loves to sew might receive a compact sewing kit, sewing machine needles, several spools of thread, a gift certificate for new patterns or material, a tracing wheel, and a box of straight pins. A sewing box to hold these new items is a wonderful alternate birthday container.

Keep the recipient's dietary restrictions in mind. For example, my aunt cannot eat chocolate, so it's not a wise choice for her basket. Ask the receiver in a matter-of-fact tone about any allergies to foods, or check with the receiver's friends or family members to ensure that the basket you make is filled with items that can be eaten rather than given away.

Enhancements run the gamut, from frosted balloons to HAPPY BIRTHDAY announcement sticks (similar to the one shown in the New Year's basket—see page 96) to horn blowers and other noisemakers. Because birthdays are such a joyous time, anything that puts a smile on the recipient's face is a gift contender. This includes items that are nostalgic, trendy, or eclectic, or anything that makes a fashion statement. Local craft and discount stores sell many items that will help you create a birthday basket the recipient will long remember.

Congratulations

An individual receives a promotion, learns a baby is due, or hears some long-awaited good news. What a great time to offer congratulations! This magenta-colored basket lined with white shred contains a wide weave, so tissue is used on the inside to hide the mechanics. Floral foam and skewers anchor the contents and help keep the bottle in place so that it doesn't sink down into the basket.

Products in this basket are snickerdoodle-flavored coffee, fortune cookies, cheese straws, vineyard-themed pasta, and a wine sauce. These items are wide and weighty, which makes this large basket a terrific choice. There's no doubt about the reason for this basket. The fortune cookies are specifically for celebration, and a sign is placed on the left side announcing the theme.

Purple is a bright and vivid color and is therefore good to use in the content's packaging, sign, and star spray enhancement. The white shred between the basket and products makes the color more evident. Purple shred was another option, but it would have darkened the gift, whereas the bed of white shred makes the purple stand out beautifully. The two enhancements, a short pick and tall star spray, add balance and beauty to this design.

Notice the tissue showing between the basket's middle knots. Inspect your design to ensure that tissue is all that's visible around the entire basket. It may not be noticeable to the recipient, but it's an exasperating feeling to notice newspaper or foam peeking through the slats. You'll have to pull the design apart to repair a problem that could have been detected earlier.

The bottle of wine sauce, which complements the pasta, is anchored using the skewering technique. For a bottle of this size, you may find that attaching two 3-inch skewers, about 1 inch apart, keeps the bottle from twisting. To secure the bottle further, curling ribbon was tied and knotted around the bottle's neck, then tied to the basket's handle. A bottle does not have to stand straight when using this method. You know it's anchored properly when it shows limited movement.

Each piece of the vineyard pasta resembles a bunch of grapes. This and other shaped pasta make wonderful alternatives to the long-and-straight type we're all so familiar with. Other shapes available in specialty stores include sports team logos, holidays, houses, and dollar signs. Shaped pasta is nutritious and flavorful, and it makes a basket appear hand-picked for the recipient.

Many products can be used to fit the congratulations category. Candy cigars, a silver-plated alphabet-block bank, an expectant-parent's log- or guidebook, and coupons for diapers or a diaper service fit a new-baby theme. Writing pads, a dictionary, healthy snacks, a laundry bag, and a roll of quarters commemorate a college acceptance letter. The congratulations basket shown here might be given to a person who's been promoted or a couple who've finalized the paperwork on a real estate investment. What better way to celebrate the start of an empire?

A person who's just purchased a new car might be congratulated with sponges, cloths, a car-wash kit, air fresheners, a steering-wheel cover, and glass cleaner, all enclosed in a pail. What do you give to someone starting a new job? Consider sparkling cider (as shown in the Good Luck basket on page 76), a key ring

The Congratulations basket.

Tissue paper lines the basket to make sure no filler shows through its open weave.

Ribbon helps keep the bottle of wine sauce securely in place.

with a success statement, a business-card holder, and a frame to place the picture of a loved one on the new desk. Breath mints are another option, though you must be careful regarding who will receive the mints and the spirit in which they're given. Some will appreciate them, and others may find them offensive.

Be aware of the recipient's preferences, and your Congratulations gift basket will be a deeply appreciated present.

Thank-You

Who says gift baskets must be big to make an impression? A thank-you gift usually isn't large. It's something that shows appreciation for kindness, such as minding the dog or feeding a fish for the weekend, collecting the mail and newspapers while out of town, or babysitting or tutoring at the last minute.

Small baskets work well for this theme, unless the appreciation is for an entire family and a large basket is appropriate. The wicker cup shown here creates a heartfelt gift that, when given, conveys complete gratitude to the recipient. The cup's inside diameter is 6 inches. Packing paper and ivory-colored shred sit atop tissue paper decorated with grapes, which lines the inner cup. Your tissue paper can be plain or printed; or you could opt not to line the cup with tissue, because the weave is tight and doesn't reveal the technique.

A few tokens of kindness are added: a Thanks a Million celebration cake, Colombian coffee, amaretto-flavored sugar, and a peach-flavored spoon. The cake takes about one minute to make in the microwave. It's mixed with water in its clear packaging and then topped with the accompanying frosting and sprinkles.

The cake also contains a balloon and candle. The teaspoon peeks over the left side of the cake.

The coffee and flavored sugar are revealed when the recipient turns the basket toward the back. Since the two items cannot be seen in the front, it's best to turn them backward so the product names are clearly viewed. This type of design is common. Many designers turn products to the side or back so that the recipient has a 360-degree view of the goodies. The tissue paper that lines the basket is taller in the back and helps pull the design together. You can make the tissue taller in the front as well. Here it's lower, so that the cake's emblem is easily seen.

Two berry picks are used, one on each side of the basket. You'll notice that most designs in this book don't show this type of balancing. If enhancements complement each other in this manner, then go ahead and add them. A stem with three plain leaves is

The Thank-You basket.

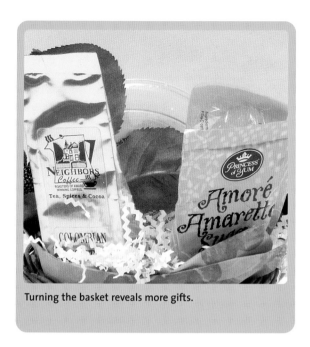
Turning the basket reveals more gifts.

added above the cake and to the back of the coffee. This piece was separated from another enhancement and was about to be discarded, but it looks nice here.

Notice that there's no top handle attached to this cup. This means that each product must be supported in one of two ways. Either make sure that the diameter is small enough to hold products snugly within the shred, or add glue dots between products to keep each item in place until the entire gift is separated.

Like many of the baskets I'll show you, this one can be presented to a man or woman. Make substitutes as needed—say, tea or cocoa rather than coffee. Other ideas for the Thank-You basket include popcorn, nuts, a notepad preprinted with the person's name, and a plush toy. You may also find fake million-dollar bills while searching through dollar stores. This fun money is great for lining the basket (instead of tissue paper), or it can be rolled, tied in the middle with curling ribbon, and inserted the same way you'd add a pick.

You'll find another design that can also be used as a thank-you offering in chapter 11—a Tote bag (see page 126). Either of these designs makes a terrific gift to show your appreciation for a job well done.

Good Luck

Here's another theme that can be created with a small or large basket, depending on the recipient and whether the contents will be enjoyed individually or shared with friends and family members. The wine basket depicted here includes a tall handle. Because the basket's weave is exposed, it's wise to place a small amount of shred on the bottom to cushion the bottle. Sparkling cider is used in this basket, but any type of bubbly is appropriate.

Added to the back are corn snacks and a tin of chocolates. The bottle hoists both items into place within the top half of the basket. Transparent tape secures the two products together at the back. Tape is also placed from each product to the outside of the basket, right below the handle. Not all baskets will allow for this type of taping, but this one features a thin weave, making it tape friendly. You can see that snack or gift items added to this design must be small and thin to share space with a tall bottle. Anything large will be too awkward to secure.

Any combination of biscotti, a two-cookie pack, sausage, cheese, or a slim package of crackers will fit in the back or sides of the basket and complement the cider. One East Coast company sells shortbread shaped to resemble horseshoes and nails—both terrific for this theme. Look for these items in specialty stores. A Tote bag can be used as a good substitute

The Good-Luck basket.

Chocolates and corn snacks are secured together with transparent tape.

A wineglass is tied to the basket's handle with ribbon.

if the depicted basket is not available.

Curling ribbon is used to tie a wineglass to the basket's handle. The glass's stem is tied first, then anchored to the handle. The position allows the top of the bottle to be inserted inside the glass, saving space and minimizing contact between the two objects. Because the bottle is wrapped in paper, there is little reason for either item to break upon contact. Your design style may lead you to anchor the glass directly at the top of the handle, which is also an acceptable choice. The embellishment, at the top left of the handle, is woven through the basket's triangular openings. Leaves and stems are wrapped around the handle, which keeps the pick in place.

Green Mardi Gras–type beads are wound around the basket, threaded through the back, and tied on one side with curling ribbon. This is a freehand method the designer created on a whim. The curling ribbon can stay long or be cut to a shorter length. You'll come up with your own unique ways to tie beads and other embellishments. The final enhancement here is a gingham-checked pull bow positioned on the basket so that the bottle's label is clearly readable.

This basket's theme is a close relative of the Congratulations gift basket, with slight variations. Good-luck wishes are offered before congratulations are extended. They're appropriate for people pursuing a quest—perhaps taking the bar exam or applying for a job that hundreds of others are applying for at the same time. The Good-Luck basket can also be presented in lieu of a congratulations gift. For example, a

Inserting the top of the cider bottle inside the glass helps prevent breakage.

Mardi Gras beads tied whimsically around the basket add a personal touch. A gingham bow completes the design.

person who gets a new job is a candidate to receive a Good-Luck basket, but the theme can be relabeled to offer congratulations. This type of versatility is something designers practice every day.

Get Well

Tea and soup are the order of the day when presenting the Get-Well basket. The sample gift shown here has been created in a bushel basket, reminiscent of the type of container you might find at a roadside fruit-and-vegetable stand. The yellow trim is bright and cheery, which makes it perfect for the theme.

This basket includes two types of soup, two types of cookies, tea, a book with tea recipes, and a honey-flavored spoon. One cookie's packaging, on the right side, includes the words GET WELL. It can't be seen, however, because the words are covered by the tea book. Still, a smile should come to the recipient's face when the cookies are revealed.

Chicken noodle soup is said to have medicinal qualities that heal a person quickly. This flavor is well known, but the brand isn't carried by supermarkets. Such a specialty should lift the receiver's spirits. She-crab soup is an alternative flavor that's popular in Southern states. The flavored spoon is made with sugar and used to sweeten tea. It dissolves into the hot beverage, leaving the spoon clean and ready for tea tasting.

This basket is packed with paper and vanilla-colored shred. Start by inserting the soup and cookies in back, which will help support the products in front. The flavored spoon was added last after the designer viewed the complete design and decided where to place it. Floral foam and skewers would also work, as long as the basket is presented to an adult who will discard the skewers responsibly.

The Get-Well basket.

Soups and teas are appropriate for the Get-Well basket.

Products are chosen to be soothing and cheerful.

The enhancements were chosen for a man or woman. Most men aren't big flower lovers, so these colors are toned down and acceptable while still attractive to women. Another consideration for a woman's design is to choose enhancements that match the basket's trim. Yellow daisies, for example, would pull the theme together. The hydrangea at the back has a long stem and is set in place by using scissors to make a narrow hole within the paper. If you have trouble keeping the stem upright, you can add a glue dot between the soup and the stem, or tape the flower's stem across the back of the soup.

One long grapevine is strung in front to add punch to the plain basket. It is attached at the rim around the silver handle. Find a point on the vine where it will grab the handle. Add an extra vine around the back if you choose.

A bushel basket isn't the only vessel to consider for this gift. An old-fashioned doctor's bag would make a wonderful container, and so would a tea cup and saucer, shown in chapter 11 (see page 134). You can also add a small tea cup and saucer within a get-well gift, as shown in the Bereavement basket in chapter 8 (see page 92). If the receiver isn't a tea drinker, try coffee, cocoa, cappuccino, or juice as a substitute. Lozenges go a long way toward healing a scratchy throat. Does the person dislike soup? Perhaps instant oatmeal with a banana is a better choice. Remember to include what the recipient prefers, not what you wish to give. That's what makes a gift memorable.

Keep in mind that fruit can be added to any gift basket design. The best place to buy fruit is at a local grocery store or specialty market where you'll select the best-looking apples, oranges, pears, grapefruits, and bananas. Only buy as much fruit as you need for

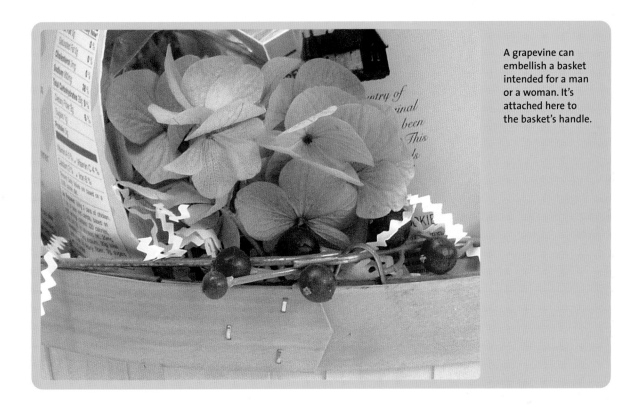

A grapevine can embellish a basket intended for a man or a woman. It's attached here to the basket's handle.

your design, which is usually no more than three of any type.

When adding fresh fruit, use a skewer to prick the cellophane at least three times after closing it around the basket. This will allow fresh air to enter the design and keep the fruit from ripening too fast. Then deliver your basket as quickly as possible so that the fruit doesn't spoil.

08

Special Themes

Change occurs over time in the lives of family members and friends. This chapter provides gift basket ideas for five recurring events that you might not have considered when giving gifts in the past. Be it a happy occasion (the purchase of a new home, the birth of a baby, a wedding) or a time for comfort (everyday stress or a death), there are many opportunities for you to express your sentiments to family and friends through a customized gift basket.

Housewarming

Good friends, new neighbors, welcome wagons, and parents who are emptying their nests all have one thing in common: Each has a reason to give a housewarming gift basket to someone who's moving into a new home, apartment, town house, or condominium.

Housewarming baskets contain a collection of functional, trendy, and whimsical items for the recipient, all depending on the new home's inhabitants. Singles, newlyweds, alternative-lifestyle couples, and traditional families with children will receive many of the same items, but there are optional products to add for each group. The basket might also include products for in-laws and pets if the family structure includes these extended members.

A flavorful rum cake, pasta shaped to resemble houses, key-lime-flavored cheese straws, wine jelly preserves, pretzels (hidden by the enhancements at the back), and key lime dip are combined to create the wonderful housewarming design shown on the next page. The basket is tall and sturdy. It's filled with packing paper and ivory-colored shred. The basket's tight weave assures that the recipient won't see the construction method, and the blue, pink, and off-white color scheme makes it a welcome addition to any household.

A berry embellishment is added in front, and a wildflower pick and star spray stand tall in the back. You can tie a bow to the handle, as shown on the right. This dual-ribbon bow of orange gingham and yellow organza enhances this attractive design and accentuates the picks' colors.

The Home Sweet Home pasta is the product that defines this basket's theme. It is easily removed and replaced with another product—a tall box of chocolates, for instance, or a large beverage bottle—to create a different theme. This gift can then be presented as a wedding present, given to a person who's just arrived home after traveling abroad, offered as comfort after a recent divorce, or created for someone who's coming home from an extended stay in the hospital. (In the latter case, be sure to consider the person's dietary restrictions when you select the products.)

Other products that work well in this basket theme are cider, drinking glasses, movie coupons, popcorn (ready-to-eat or microwave), tortilla chips, salsa,

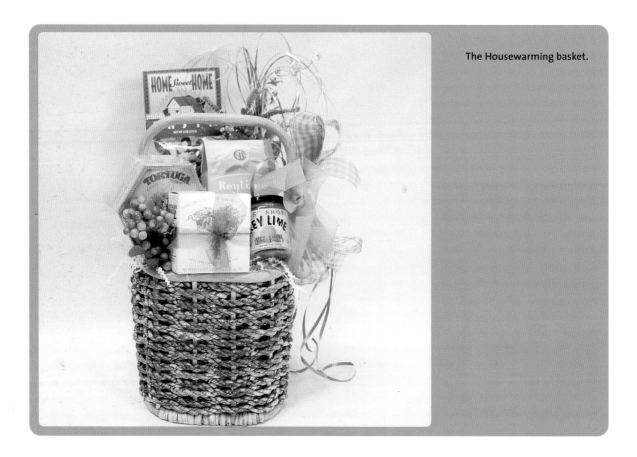

The Housewarming basket.

pasta sauce, bread sticks, a wall plaque, utensils, stationery, kitchen magnets, key rings, mugs, the recipient's city or state official magazine, a bill organizer, a homeowner's journal (as shown in the Wedding basket; see page 90), and a coupon holder.

If you're adding drinking glasses, the stems can be tied onto the handle in the same manner as shown for the Good-Luck (page 76) and New Year's Day (page 96) baskets. Be sure to secure the two glasses by placing a glue dot between them. That will prevent friction, which might otherwise increase the likelihood of breakage.

Another charming treatment for this design is to use a basket shaped like a house. If you can find such a vessel, there's no need for products that state WELCOME HOME or HOME SWEET HOME. The container's shape will designate the theme. Box containers are also available with house designs stenciled on the front, which is another option. Or try using a dish drainer, umbrella stand, or mesh waste container. Men will appreciate a toolbox or food-tray table as the container for their housewarming gift.

This basket's contents and alternatives highlight how many products are interchangeable according to the recipient's preferences. Keep this in mind to create a cozy Housewarming basket.

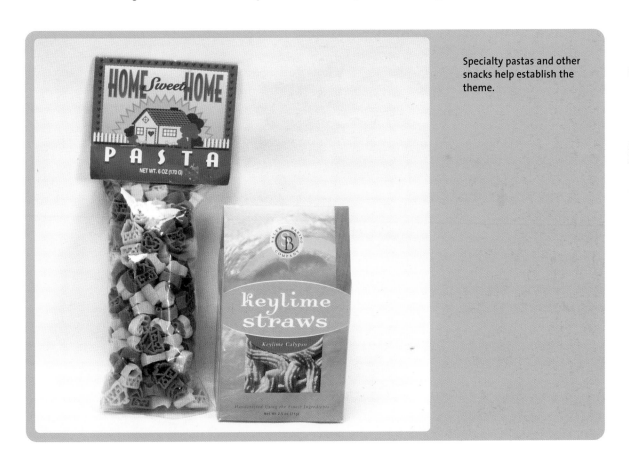

Specialty pastas and other snacks help establish the theme.

Baby

Creating a basket to welcome a newborn is an exciting task, and it's also filled with challenges. There are many items that you will find to add to this design, so you must plan what to buy ahead of time, or the gift will be as big as a nursery when you're finished! With this in mind, here's a look at three designs that welcome the new baby to the world and a variety of alternate products that stand alone or can be added within each basket.

The first design (Baby basket I) uses a container carryall that's nicknamed the "Moses basket." It's a soft baby carrier with sun bonnet on top and handles on each side. A round mobile toy is attached at the top of the bonnet. This container also includes a matching protective cover that zips the container closed on the bottom half. The cover was removed to fill the basket with baby items. This design contains a plush bear, picture frame with a small bear attached on top, a soft white blanket, baby hanger, tote bag, booties, bottle, photo album, matching plate and cup, handprint kit, and piggy bank.

The handprint kit and combination plate and cup are printed with the words, MY FIRST BIRTHDAY. Both are appropriate to add to a newborn's gift for future use. Each is an item that proud parents will look forward to using as their child grows in the coming year. The white blanket drapes outside and down the front of the basket. It's added here to give you a better look at the item. It can be folded or rolled before you wrap the basket. The space under the bonnet is a good location for the blanket. It's also appropriate to keep the blanket in its original packaging so that the item stays clean.

Baby basket I: The Moses basket.

Insert a bear, bottle, bank, booties, and more to welcome the new baby.

Packing paper is the best choice as a filler material. Floral foam will also hold items steady, but its gritty texture, along with pointed skewers, may seem out of place for a baby gift. In addition, newsprint will soil the basket's inner lining. This container's pink and white colors are primarily for a girl; however, this

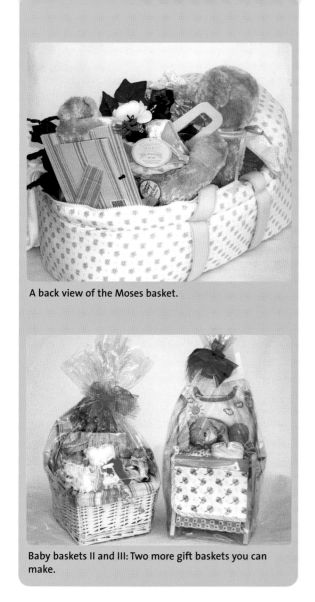

A back view of the Moses basket.

Baby baskets II and III: Two more gift baskets you can make.

the theme and as double protection against shifting. Enhancements are added last as a finishing touch. Greenery is in between products, but you may decide to add baby-themed picks to complement your design.

Other items that are appreciated by new parents include nail clippers, soap and lotion, diapers, a night-light, diaper wipes, a comb and brush, a teething ring, and a lullaby CD. This basket is filled with great items for baby. Gifts for Mom and Dad are also appropriate. Consider products such as new-parent books and burping cloths.

The Moses basket is one of many containers available for a baby gift. A traditional woven basket, as used by the women who assembled a baby basket in 1913 (see page 4), is another candidate. Other options include a diaper pail, bathing tub, child's wagon, stroller, or compact changing station.

You can change the look of your gift by substituting a traditional basket or laundry container (Baby baskets II and III). The wicker basket is lined with striped fabric. It's a warm and inviting addition for any baby design. A generous helping of white tissue shred elevates the products. Shred is a better choice than newsprint to elevate items due to its specific theme. This basket includes a washcloth, two teething rings, a bottle, a picture frame with a small bear peeking above the top edge, and a photo album. It's closed in clear cellophane and topped with a bow. This design also looks great encased in a basket bag or shrink wrap.

The laundry container is a darling vessel to choose as your design foundation. Can you imagine the look on the parents' faces when they see it? Like the wicker-basket gift, this one is also filled with white

basket is available in blue for boys or white if the baby's gender is unknown. The packing paper is topped with pink tissue, and the gift items are set in the natural grooves made by the paper. Glue dots are helpful to keep items upright. Add them sparingly. When all items are in place, shred is added on top of the pink tissue, between each product, to complete

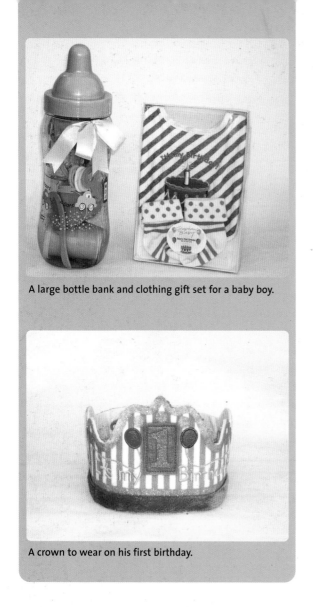

A large bottle bank and clothing gift set for a baby boy.

A crown to wear on his first birthday.

Other products to consider in either basket are pacifiers, child-protection locks, socks, bath wash, and lotion. Some of these items are shown here, such as pacifiers inside a large bottle that doubles as a bank.

These baskets only scratch the surface of what's available for the new baby and new parents. Narrow your choices to include unique yet practical items that the parents are less likely to receive from other gift givers. Team these with great containers such as the ones shown here, and you'll create a gift basket that will be treasured for a lifetime.

Spa Treatment

Everyone loves to be pampered. Who wouldn't want to receive a collection of exotic soaps, scrubs, and scents? Few will purchase them for themselves, however, which is why the Spa basket (also called the Pamper basket by veteran designers) is a popular gift for any occasion and gender. It can be given to say thank-you, as a stress reliever or housewarming gift, for Mother's or Father's Day, or to a person who deserves a little downtime after a hectic event.

A large, round basket was chosen to create the contemporary design shown here. A smaller vessel is just as effective, especially when a petite thank-you or housewarming gift is appropriate. No floral foam or skewers are used here. The inner walls contain enough packing paper to fill and elevate the products and enhancements. White and gold shred is placed on top of the paper before items are added.

Select products according to how the recipient prefers to be pampered. Some individuals love baths, while others head for the shower. Does the person have access to a spa, whirlpool, or sauna? If the recipient lives in a climate where sandals are the preferred

tissue shred to support the gifts within its opening. Included are a plush dog, bottle, bib, washcloth, and booties. A bib is elevated behind the container. It creates an attractive backdrop. The cardboard in the bib's original packaging is the prop that displays it behind the laundry vessel. It's best to close this special gift in cellophane or a basket bag. Shrink wrapping has a tendency to distort the bib's position.

The Spa basket.

Add lotions, candles, and skin softeners for all-day pampering.

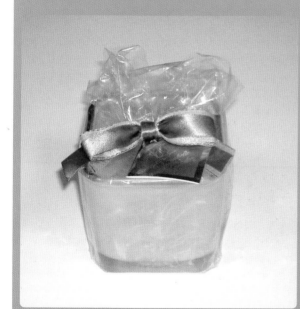

A close-up of the candle packaged in glass.

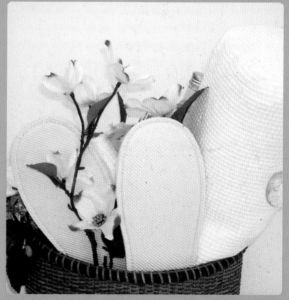

Consider adding a bath pillow and slippers.

foot gear, foot lotion will be appreciated. What about bath products that make lots of bubbles, and how about adding candles? Is the person allergic to certain fragrances? Think about all these options before deciding on what will create the ultimate pampering pleasure.

This bountiful basket holds soaps, lotions, bath cubes, a scented candle, spa slippers, and a bath pillow. Bath cubes are small, so cubes in a variety of scents are added between the flowers and other floral enhancements. Star spray or ting-ting would make a nice presentation, but this design is filled with white flowers low in front and high in back. Floral tissue paper facing upward around the basket's rim, as shown in the Thanksgiving basket (see page 119) is an attractive option if creating a man's spa basket.

Some candles are purchased without cellophane wrapping, and others are prewrapped and topped with a bow. The latter is how this square container candle was bought. It's your decision whether or not to wrap jar, tapered, or votive candles before insertion. When you wrap candles, it's as if the item becomes a gift within a gift. Recipients love unwrapping every part of their basket, so consider wrapping gift items as part of the gift experience. Do what experienced designers do: Use leftover cellophane to wrap candles and other small items, and tie it at the top with a small bow made from regular or curling ribbon in a color that complements the gift. The technique also serves to protect the candles from items that may scar them while in transit.

The white slippers and pillow are appropriate for a man's or woman's spa basket and can be found in other colors to suit the recipient's preference. Inserting the slippers takes a few minutes of ingenuity.

Before adding, you may decide to angle them slightly in a cross method at midpoint or place them in the basket straight and upright, close to each other as shown here. Either method works well and looks attractive. Also, it's suggested that you position the slippers and pillow before adding other items. This is best because other gift items will be disrupted by the procedure. Use your fingers or scissors to gently move the packing paper away from the inside of the basket where the slippers will be inserted. This creates a temporary small space. Add the slippers, bringing them down halfway into the basket. Release the paper so that it presses and holds the slippers in place. Adjust the slippers as needed.

Bath pillows are rarely prefilled with air, so completion of this design requires you to blow air into the pillow or use an air pump to inflate it. The pillow need not be completely filled with air. The bottom portion, which is tucked into the basket in the same manner as the slippers, is inflated just enough to ensure that the top portion looks attractive. It will take you several tries to get the appearance you desire, but the results will be worth the effort. This pillow includes two suction cups for a firm connection in the bathtub. Only one is visible above the basket; the other is tucked below.

Adding flowers or shred between the pillow and slippers is an option. None is shown in this design, except for the tall branch of flowers behind one slipper. Tissue paper is another alternative. You'll also notice that one floral branch is added in one slipper's midsection, soon to be replaced by the recipient's toes. It's a technique that is sometimes overlooked while designing. Take advantage of every area within the gift basket to add beauty and dazzle.

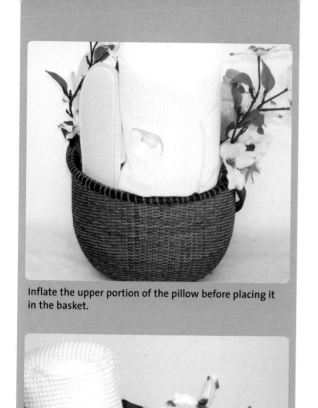
Inflate the upper portion of the pillow before placing it in the basket.

The slipper's toe area is a good place for enhancements.

When you think about spa baskets, you also dream of eating chocolates and drinking a bubbly beverage. While a beverage is appropriate to add, it's wise not to tuck chocolates between soaps or scented products. Chocolates, in any form, will absorb the stronger scents and become unpalatable. Consider adding food items in another basket or simply pre-

senting the snacks as an additional gift. Try this experiment if you wish to add foods to a spa basket. Wrap the food in separate cellophane, and then wrap the entire basket together. Wait a few days. Unwrap the basket, and taste the foods. If there's no trace of the scented items, you're cleared to present the same basket to another person. Designers nationwide play it safe by keeping foods away from spa products.

Other containers to consider for this design include miniature porcelain or plastic tubs, brass buckets, and shower caddies.

Wedding

One wedding has the ability to keep your hands immersed in shred for days. Not only will you make a basket for the bride and groom, but other members of the wedding party are candidates to receive bridal party baskets. That includes the bridesmaids, men's party, mothers of the bride and groom, and the wedding planner. Still, your creativity can make $100 gift certificates pale in comparison.

A picnic basket was chosen to create this lovely gift. Its large size will come in handy when the newlyweds decide to enjoy sandwiches, snacks, and a sparkling beverage on a warm afternoon or late summer's night. This basket contains a scone mix, nonalcoholic cider, a scented candle wrapped in tulle, embroidered toilet tissue, a homeowner's journal, cookies, white cheddar popcorn, wine jelly, four goblets, and red-roasted-pepper jam. Notice the placement of the burgundy-colored table runner draped in front of the basket. It helps break up the white color and adds warmth to the design.

As with most basket designs in this book, packing paper and shred form the bottom foundation. The linen table runner lies flat within the inner front wall of the basket and is doubled in the front. There are many products within this basket, but depending on the couple's preferences, others can either be added or substituted. For example, if the couple met while traveling, postcards and other items that remind them of their initial meeting add a sentimental touch. For couples who share a love for photography, photo frames and photographic cleaning supplies show your thoughtfulness. Consider what the couple has in common, and include it among the snacks and gifts.

This basket is best adorned with the bridal party's colors, so make sure you know the palette ahead of time. The colors can be highlighted within the shred, embellishments, cellophane closure (unless a clear wrap is used), and some of the products' packages. Such a basket can be presented to the bride during the bridal shower or to celebrate an anniversary.

The handle on the bottom of the basket (below) loops around another handle on top, which secures the basket when it's being carried. The four goblets are held in place by white ribbon strung across the

The Wedding basket.

In this Wedding basket, one goblet holds a tulle-wrapped candle . . .

. . . while another contains roasted-red-pepper jam.

Embroidered toilet tissue and a journal are suitable gifts for the bride and groom.

four inside corners of the basket. Each goblet sits comfortably and can be filled with shred or a small product, unless you prefer to leave the glasses empty. The goblet on the left is a perfect fit for the scented candle wrapped in tulle. The goblet on the right holds the jam. This use of space gives the basket a full appearance. Aside from the linen, only one embellishment is used, which can be seen on the right in the lid. Fewer enhancements make the products the focal point. However, consider styling your basket with the types of embellishments that add glamour and beauty—include the type of "flora and fauna" that celebrate the day's union.

Embroidery, as shown on the toilet tissue, adds a touch of elegance to a product that's known more for its functionality. Consider the first letter of the couple's last name as an embroidered touch on something you add to a basket. The homeowner's journal is a thoughtful item for every couple to document valuables, mementos, and changes in their home over the years.

Smaller baskets for the bridal party might include personalized or engraved items, bubbles and a wand, lotions, foot soaks and sprays (to soothe their feet after the festivities), and a picture frame to hold the bridal-party picture. The maid or matron of honor's basket can include the same items plus another special gift. Her basket is created with a slightly different color scheme than the rest of the bridal party. Use special ribbon imprinted with a wedding wish or other sentiment to close these gifts after applying cellophane or shrink wrap.

Bereavement

Gift baskets are associated with joyous events, but the Bereavement basket takes a detour from celebratory giving. This basket's mission is to bring comfort to one or more persons who have lost a loved one. Not only is it given when a close relative passes, but it is also becoming an accepted gift to offer when a pet departs. If you browse through greeting cards, you will notice that the pet card section is increasing in size. That's a strong indicator of how important gifts for grieving pet companions have become.

This beautifully tailored gift is contained in a small, dark red basket filled with packing paper and ivory-colored shred. The rim is sprayed with a brushed gold paint. Much like the Thank-You basket (see page 74), this gift does not have to be large in size to convey the sentiment. Included are two coffees, tea, lemon curd mix, an apple-flavored spoon, a small cup and saucer, a gold-plated spoon, a picture frame, and a linen napkin. The embellishment tastefully incorporates delicate flowers and a butterfly.

Notice that the handle is positioned from front to back, whereas the Good-Luck basket's handle (see page 76) is side to side. A glue dot is added between the cup and saucer, which keeps the pair from breaking due to pressure or rough handling while in transit. The linen napkin was added to the basket before the other items so that one side would sit flat along the basket's inner wall. Your napkin does not have to be angled in this position. Arrange it in a way that flatters the basket and its contents. Notice how shred is visible on the left side while being absent on the other due to the napkin's inclusion. It proves that a basket can look beautiful without symmetry.

This Bereavement basket is an asymmetrical design with a linen napkin on the right and shred on the left.

The cup and saucer are secured with a glue dot.

The second coffee, a chocolate mint flavor, is not visible until you turn the basket backward and see the coffee directly behind the lemon curd mix. You don't have to place products in back, as done here, but it is a good use of space. The idea was simply to add another beverage option for the recipient. The primary color scheme (green, white, and red) also influenced the addition of a second coffee.

Frames are added to many bereavement baskets. During this grieving period, frames are not a priority to the recipient, but it will be considered a thoughtful gesture to house a picture of the departed. A frame size of 3 by 5 or 4 by 6 inches is appropriate for a small or medium basket. Coffee and tea are known for their comforting qualities, but as with all designs, recipients should receive their preferred beverage. For the lemon curd mix, you might substitute a mix for scones or other breads. Shortbread or chocolate chip cookies, biscotti, lemon straws, a small cake, and individually wrapped hard candies are excellent options as well.

Many gift items, such as the frame and cup-and-saucer combination, are available for this basket. Cards and envelopes for thank-you notes, poem books, and flower seeds make thoughtful inclusions. While baskets are terrific vessels, also consider small multi-colored boxes, such as shown in chapter 10, or a flower pot, especially if you're adding seeds.

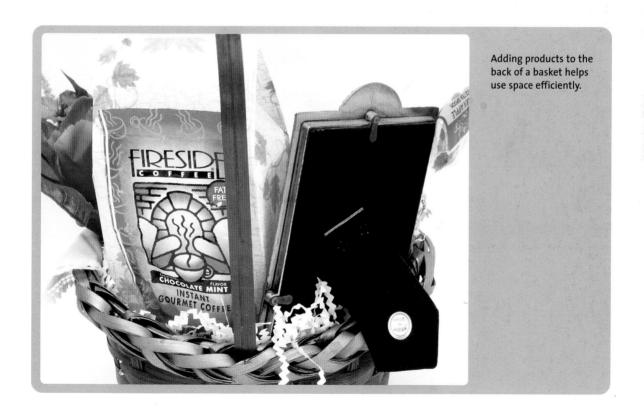

Adding products to the back of a basket helps use space efficiently.

If you plan to ship this gift to another state, be sure to wrap the tea cup and saucer individually in bubble wrap, which is available at any office supply store. The items can be reinserted into the basket after the protective wrapping is added. Frames must also be wrapped so the glass won't break. Shrink wrap is the preferred closure method for shipping. Often, however, designers use a double layer of cellophane around the gift in place of shrink wrap before packing it for shipping.

Bereavement baskets may not be a gift you'll make often, but each design created with your loving hands will soothe the receiver in the difficult days ahead.

09 Celebrating Holidays

Sharing Love, Laughter, and Tradition

Searching through malls to find the right gift for someone who has it all or is just starting to amass a fortune isn't an easy task. That's why buying a collection of small items to make a custom gift basket serves two functions: It lets your creative genius shine through, and it thrills the receiver with a gift that's made especially for him or her. Look at these designs for inspiration to create your own special occasion baskets.

New Year's Day

Most people love January 1. It's a day to start anew and resolve to do better in life, both personally and professionally. That's what this New Year's basket reflects. After a night of revelry or a quiet evening at home watching the ball drop in Times Square, many feel that this is the time to "clean up their act." That includes anything from reducing their weight to starting a business to ending nonhealthy habits. This basket focuses on setting goals while providing the receiver with a good breakfast to enjoy while pondering how to live better in the new year.

Look for light, cheerful colors to celebrate the event. A large, white-washed basket separated into four inner sections houses this New Year's design. One section is divided lengthwise in the front, while the three remaining sections are in back. Cutting floral foam would have been too complex for this basket, so packing paper and purple-colored shred have been used for product support.

A gold-and-white table runner was doubled before insertion and draped over the basket's front in a triangular shape. Some designers roll place mats, runners, and napkins, tying them in the middle with curling ribbon and inserting them into the basket along with the other products. A great time to buy these items printed with the words HAPPY NEW YEAR is between January and March when stores discount such products in hopes of recouping their money. Dollar stores may also sell such items early in the year.

This package represents goodies to eat for breakfast and items for healthy snacking while the recipient plans yearly goals and aspirations. In the front row are blueberry syrup, buttermilk pancake mix, peach cobbler syrup, and lemon straws. The back includes a large bottle of Bloody Mary mix, a scone mix, and white cheddar popcorn. The handle sup-

ports two glasses secured with purple curling ribbon. The glasses are tied together in such a way that neither will touch the other. If the glasses were closer, a glue dot would be placed between them to prevent breakage.

New Year's Day is one of the few times that a diet pig wand (shown below), will be appreciated and taken in the spirit in which it's given. In other words, the recipient is likely to see it as a fun gift and not one implying that the person needs to lose weight. The wand includes instructions that tell the receiver to wave it over each meal and snack to remove all calories. A HAPPY NEW YEAR pick sits on the left side within the basket's weave. Such picks serve to name the bas-

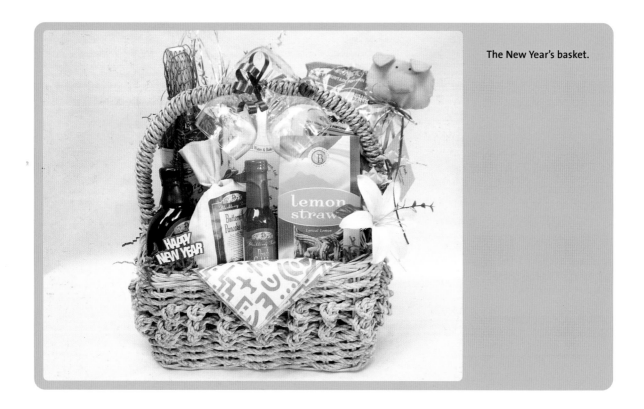

The New Year's basket.

ket without additional indication from any of the products. This design is also terrific for birthday, thank-you, congratulations, and a dozen more themes. All you need is a small pick similar to the one for New Year's to state the purpose. Other embellishments include a flower pick on the right and a silver star spray in back between the two mixes. These enhancements show how to embellish without overpowering the products.

Resolutions play a big part in determining what to put into a New Year's basket, as well as the person's lifestyle, marital status, and recreational activities. Consider adding journals, healthy snacks, travel aids, store gift certificates, and magazines. Inverted top hats and fabric-covered boxes are two of the many containers that also make a great presentation.

I once showed a New Year's gift basket on The Food Network using many of these same items fastened to an oval-shaped silver serving tray. Cardboard covered with tissue paper sat within the tray to protect it from scarring. Each product was set alongside the others, which served to keep all products upright. Embellishments were added to small pieces of floral foam covered with tissue. The foam was fastened to the cardboard with glue dots. Designing with flat trays takes more time than traditional baskets, but it can make a wonderful gift that the recipient will recall the following New Year's Day.

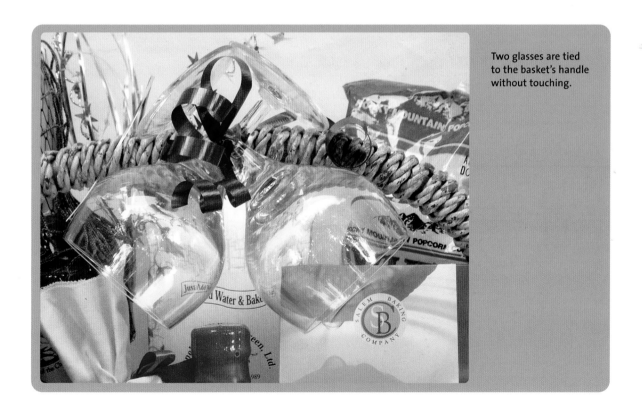

Two glasses are tied to the basket's handle without touching.

Valentine's Day

There's a group of women in Illinois who make gift baskets only during special holidays. Valentine's Day is one of these holidays. About a month before February 14, the women visit every discount store in the region, gathering as many low-cost items as possible. When the baskets are ready, they're sold at the busiest intersections.

Men are the biggest targets, because they usually wait until the last minute to buy a gift. And they don't buy just one: They'll select baskets for a spouse or girlfriend, mother, mother-in-law, aunt, and grandmother. Pricing their baskets at $20 to $25 each, these enterprising women make thousands of dollars in less than a week. It's a lot of work, but the payoff is worth the hours it takes to make a product that sells quickly.

Valentine's Day is one of the three most popular occasions to buy a gift basket. While some individuals stay true to the standard box of chocolates, others prefer to find items that evoke passion, show affection, or rekindle a relationship. Each year manufacturers create romantic new products to pair with old favorites, some of which are shown in this delightful Valentine's Day design.

This medium-sized oval basket is sprayed red and trimmed with a gold border. It's packed with paper and topped in red-colored shred. Love and Kisses shortbread cookies are surrounded by "Hot Hunk" beef jerky, wild-cherry-flavored body frosting, chocolate calligraphy (with paintbrush and instructions written on an attached scroll), passion mood chocolates, a Valentine's Day poem book, lover's tea bags, and a Love Map, which highlights the history of the world's great lovers. The body frosting is made to top

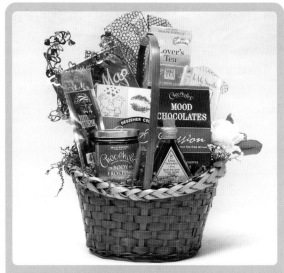

The Valentine's Day basket.

ice cream or fruit. Like the chocolate calligraphy, it can also be painted onto a person's body.

Here's an example of star spray that's available in a shape other than stars on a wire. This embellishment contains filled and open hearts that were wrapped around a thick marker to create circular shapes. A rose and baby's-breath pick are inserted on the right, and a bow made with punchinello ribbon is added at the back. The bow was made with a Bowdabra machine, available at many craft stores. Punchinello is a very forgiving ribbon. This same bow traveled in my suitcase to Dallas, Los Angeles, and Chicago before I added it to this design. It lay between my clothes, flat as a Frisbee, and still looks great.

Exotic goodies aren't the only products to include for that special someone. Low-cost treats continue to be Valentine's Day favorites. Red Hots, Hershey's Kisses, Fireballs, and heart-shaped candies imprinted with messages make terrific gifts. Boxes of chocolate fit snugly into many small and medium-sized baskets. Gifts such as the Love Map and poem book are wonderful complements. Heart-shaped sponges or pillows, massage or day spa certificates, a CD of love songs, and heart-shaped picture frames lovingly cómplete this basket. Also consider giving the Spa basket, shown in chapter 8 (see page 87), for Valentine's Day. An ice bucket, heart-shaped box, or anything made with brass makes a great container if a basket isn't grand enough.

My second guest appearance on The Food Network was to show Valentine's Day gifts. Most items had to be foods, of course, but I added some unique gift items among the edibles. I showed gifts made on silver serving trays, in a heart-shaped red pocketbook made from cardboard, and on an oval brass container similar to what Godiva uses for its deluxe cookie tin. One gift, made specifically for an expectant mother, was com-

posed of cookies, biscotti, and tea tucked into a mug made in the shape of a pregnant woman's stomach. It might sound strange, but it was a big hit with the show hosts and individuals who called to order. Left-over mugs were made into Mother's Day gifts.

Remember to look for plush animals for your Valentine's Day baskets. One of my best sellers was a "Prisoner of Love" dog. It was white with black stripes, had a dark circle around its left eye, a ball and chain on one ankle, and a white prison shirt with an inmate's number on the back. The dog was one item I could never keep enough of in stock. People bought it individually and for basket inclusion. Unfortunately, the company that made it stopped production.

A Valentine's Day basket is a very personal gift that expresses the world's most powerful emotion. Choose your products carefully, and the creation will express sentiments better than a box of chocolates.

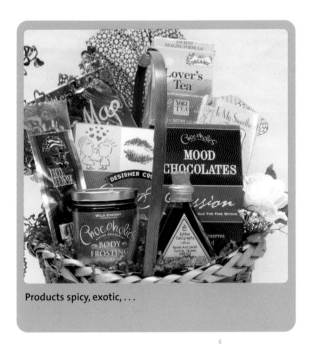

Products spicy, exotic, . . .

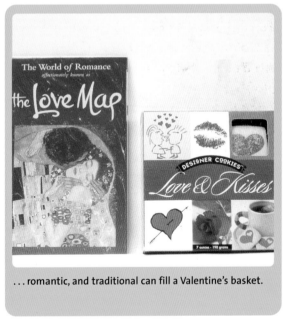

. . . romantic, and traditional can fill a Valentine's basket.

Mother's Day

There are times when a traditional basket is enough to create a Mother's Day design. Other times, however, you must have a container that's as unique as the woman who will receive it. The wooden wheelbarrow for the design shown here was chosen because Mom is in charge of 99 percent of household duties. Therefore, she needs an extra pair of hands or at least a vessel that represents a friendly helper. I remember the days when my arms were filled with my daughter, two bags of groceries, and an umbrella. A wheelbarrow would have been dandy.

This container is a candidate for either packing paper or floral foam. The choice depends on how deep the products are within the wheelbarrow and if anything is in danger of tipping out before it's wrapped. This design uses tissue-wrapped floral foam and green-colored shred. Several products require skewers. The open weave requires you to place tissue paper along the inside of the basket before adding the filling. This tissue is printed with spring flowers, enhancing the garden theme that the wheelbarrow also represents.

Inside this basket are an easy-to-make pasta dinner, corn snacks, peanut brittle, cookies, crackers, two types of wine jelly, cheese spread, and an imprinted mug. Long-stemmed yellow roses are added on the right, and faux green grapes sit between the products

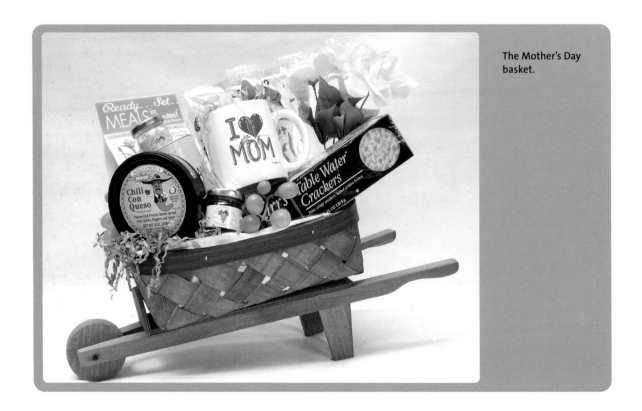

The Mother's Day basket.

in the front and on the left. The mug contains flowers that were made by my daughter, Genesis, for a school project. Alternate mug items are tea or other beverage of Mom's choice, cookies, or hard candies.

One jar of wine jelly is stacked atop the cookie can; two glue dots keep the jelly in place. The pasta meal and corn snacks are tucked into the space between the wheelbarrow and floral foam. There's no need for skewers, as used with the other products. Mugs are flat and easily added to most designs. Glue dots help hold the mug in place on top of the crackers. An alternative location for the mug is where the cheese spread stands, leaving the spread to be added atop the crackers.

Your product selection should encourage Mom to relax and enjoy the day. It may not be possible, especially with today's hectic pace, but the thought will be appreciated. This is an occasion where items that Mom truly loves should be the only products included. Look for stationery, writing instruments, and journals if she writes personal notes or jots down ideas. An organizer that keeps these items in one place is a potential container. Is she a collector of lace or figurines? Consider adding that type of gift. Perhaps baking is her passion. Cookie cutters, a cake plate (potential container), a matching apron and mitt, a recipe book, and parchment paper are possibilities to include on your list. If she's ready for a handheld

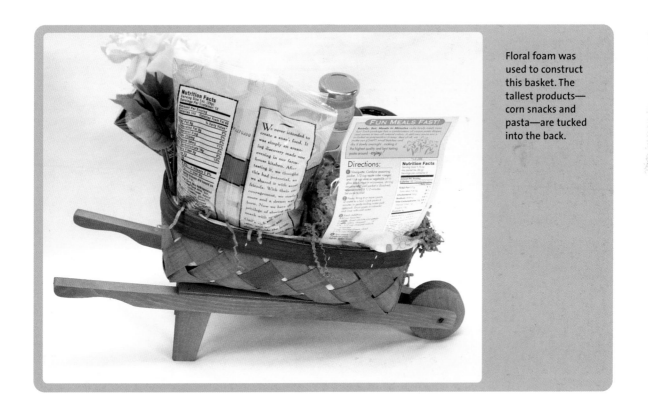

Floral foam was used to construct this basket. The tallest products—corn snacks and pasta—are tucked into the back.

organizer, they're available for low prices and are small enough to fit in her purse. What about the professional mom? Personalized luggage tags, a monogrammed business-card holder, a travel alarm clock, a wallet to hold her passport, and other valuables will be appreciated.

A hat box is another container she'll treasure. It's destined to be a keepsake item, such as the one made with brocade fabric and velveteen used to create the Chocoholics basket in chapter 10 (see page 122). This is another container that was a customer favorite. One person ordered six Mother's Day baskets using the hat box. Each was filled with candles, perfumes, soaps, drawer and closet sachets, room fresheners, bubble bath, lotions, and heart-shaped mirrors, all with a specific fragrance for each recipient. Flowers that corresponded with the scents lined the box. The gifts were shipped as far as the Canary Islands, so the arrangements were shrink-wrapped and covered with printed cellophane to make a dazzling presentation.

Another person wanted a gift basket for a mom who loves lottery scratch-off tickets. He gave me a hundred tickets and asked that I make what he called a "basket of luck." I wrapped each ticket in cellophane and attached them all to individual skewers. The tickets looked like lollipops, which I inserted into floral foam. The cellophane was closed with an enormous bow and a card that read, "I'm lucky to have you as a mom."

This special lady screamed with joy when I delivered the basket on Mother's Day. She invited me into her home and immediately called her son. Her voice stayed at a high pitch—so much so that a neighbor alerted the police. They arrived soon after, but the woman never calmed down. She invited the police

inside to see her basket of luck. I was ready to leave to spend the day with my own mom, but as luck would have it, one of the policemen asked if I could make the same gift for his own mother, with the addition of coffee and scones. It takes a while to wrap individual lottery tickets, so his gift was delivered the next day. Mother's Day gift baskets are a joy to create, and it's wonderful to get a glimpse of the love between a mother and her children.

Make Mom's favorite things the focal point of your search, and don't stop until you find the items she adores. Her reaction will be worth it.

Father's Day

Making a Father's Day gift seems easier than creating one for Mother's Day. That's because most retail stores treat all dads the same way. They've convinced cus-

The Father's Day basket.

This Father's Day basket focuses on that men's favorite: open-and-eat snacks. Few embellishments are needed, though cattails and a wildflower pick add interest.

no matter where Dad lives, be it in a rural or city setting. The laid-back lifestyle of many dads means that floral foam and skewers aren't needed here. Although the basket contains several openings within the weave, tissue paper wasn't a necessity. The brown packing paper topped with purple-colored shred corresponded well with this design.

I never met a man who didn't want to tear away the cellophane and dive into flavorful snacks. If this sounds like your husband, dad, or other significant male, this basket is for him.

The basket contains a beef-steak stick, caramel popcorn, seasoned nuts, combination beef jerky and cheese sticks, dipping pretzels, mustard, and a beer bread mix in a tall glass bottle. The mix is simple to make and can be served during Father's Day dinner.

A favorite beverage, disposable camera to capture the day's festivities, a mug, sports video, a pouch to hold the remote control and television guide, grooming tools, a car-wash kit, and a picture frame to place a family photo are other options for Dad's basket. As with a basket for Mom, adding his preferences is important to make the day special. Perhaps he favors a certain fragrance that's available as a soap, cologne, after-shower spray, and powder. That makes a marvelous basket, but as with other designs, don't combine these items in the same basket with food. Either give Dad two small baskets separated by items to eat and items for grooming, or select just one group of many items that can be paired together.

Basket substitutes run the gamut. A toolbox, snack bowl, car organizer, decorative wastebasket for his favorite area, and bucket for car washing provide ample room for gift placement. I've created Father's Day baskets for busy executives using open briefcases

tomers that dads should receive ties, money clips, cologne, a pack of briefs, socks, and that square piece of wood on which keys and spare change are placed. Most dads won't balk at receiving these items, but with gift baskets, you can do much better.

Some dads are happy on this special day to tinker around their favorite toys—cars, wide-screen televisions, a pool table, or a variety of electronic gadgets. Others get together with friends they haven't seen in months. Then there are the dads who are content to stand guard over a grill after almost destroying the kitchen during preparation.

Many men, though, are fans of open-and-eat foods, and that's the focus of this Father's Day basket. A rectangular country basket with green trim provides the foundation and makes an attractive appearance filled with writing instruments, notepads, an anti-stress toy, several business magazines, a business-card holder, and bags of healthy snacks.

You'll notice that this basket isn't filled with many enhancements. Most men aren't fans of frills. They're excited about the snacks and gifts, not "flora and fauna." This design is limited to two cattails and a small wildflower pick that matches the shred's color. Don't add much more than this to your Father's Day basket unless the recipient appreciates embellishments.

Designers don't receive as many calls for Dad's Day baskets as they do for Mother's Day, but they stay prepared for the few orders received. Their inventory includes a variety of sweet, savory, and peppery products that are normally added to all-occasion baskets. Fishing-box and tool-caddy baskets are purchased by real estate salesmen and relocation specialists who thank their clients using containers that match recipients' lifestyles. They learn a lot about customers through the initial prequalification meetings and subsequent gatherings. When designers find a bargain on baskets and containers that create good-looking men's designs, they buy a collection knowing that both individuals and corporate buyers will order.

Men are seldom choosy when it comes to basket contents. As long as you include a collection of great-tasting foods, he'll award you with "two thumbs up," meaning the basket is a winner.

July 4th

It starts with a hot summer day made hotter by the mandatory grill-cooked hamburgers and a kettle of baked beans. But then you reach into the basket of summer snacks that arrived yesterday. It's complete with assorted lemonade mixes, homemade peanut brittle, lemon-slice candies, buttery popcorn, and an assortment of penny candies that remind you of your childhood. The children race through the backyard, playing with the pinwheels and blowing bubbles that were also stashed in the basket. As you grab a slice of watermelon and press a cold glass of lemonade to your forehead, you think about the evening's festivities, sitting in a lounge chair and watching the fireworks from your second-floor balcony with that basket of snacks at your fingertips.

Independence Day stands out as a significant holiday for Americans. Wars abroad and tragic circumstances in New York, Washington, D.C., and Pennsylvania have in recent years helped place more focus on family ties and taking nothing in our lives for granted. American memorabilia in country and contemporary styles is a big business, which makes creating a July 4th gift basket as simple as blowing on a pinwheel. Red, white, and blue are colors you'll find in lots of product packaging. That's another fact that makes finding appropriate products easy.

The basket depicted here is crafted to resemble a boat. It's curved on both sides and contains feet on the bottom as if the basket is in permanent dry dock. The handles fall to the sides and help augment the container. Because of the curved bottom, it's easier to place red-colored shred on top of packing paper rather than making a mess by cutting floral foam into shape.

A mix of "eat now, make later" products can be used to fill this basket. A shrimp dip, peanut brittle, corn snacks, cookies, clam dip kit, snack mix, grill seasonings, assorted beverages, and a flavored teaspoon proudly represent the day. Rather than use glue dots to keep each product upright, an extra layer of

Shaped to resemble a boat, this vessel makes a great foundation for a Fourth of July gift basket.

A mix of "eat now, make later" products will come in handy at a July 4th picnic.

to consider for this design. Look for a horn or bugle, a CD of patriotic music, a Statue of Liberty figurine, small packages of apple pie, American-themed bumper stickers, historic books, toy pinwheels for the children, and thong slippers. An upturned top hat makes a good container, as would a ceramic watermelon bowl or apple pie plate.

My designing friends in the Southern California area are pros at making July 4th baskets using tabletop barbecue grills as the container. The grills, which are sold for less than $5 each, are purchased from local drugstores that sell each with utensils and squirt bottles for ketchup, mustard, and relish. Once one drugstore's stock is depleted, they move on to others within the chain, grabbing grills until the summer ends or the inventory is gone, whichever comes first. Not only do customers order these custom creations for relatives whom they cannot visit during the holiday, but the designers also receive many orders from workers in the home construction and decorating industries.

A July 4th basket can be combined with summer items such as plates, bowls, cups, and napkins. These products are usually placed at the back of the basket, while the snacks sit in front. Barbecue sauces, corncob holders, an ice cream scooper, cones, and toppings are summertime fixings that also create a great design. Super Soakers, bat and balls, and jump ropes are fun toys to add for children, as long as each is safe for the targeted age group.

Independence Day has a different meaning for every person, and gift baskets are versatile enough to incorporate something for everyone. Try creating one that's patriotic and another that encompasses the meaning of summer. You'll make someone's turn at the grill a lot easier.

shred holds each product in place. Try setting a plastic election campaign hat atop the products, fastened with glue dots. It's an item that you may have in your basement or attic waiting for a great basket design to adorn. Add two star sprays made with white onion grass and red and blue stars. Small flags are another enhancement that will fit the occasion.

Patriotic items are perfect, but there's much more

Christmas

A Christmas basket has the power to make an adult race alongside the children to see what's under the tree. I know one woman who, after receiving a gift basket in 1994, doesn't feel the holiday is complete without getting at least one basket of gifts. It might be placed under the tree, or a relative could be charged with bringing it to the dinner festivities. She'll even allow the use of the same basket, as long as it's filled with a few trinkets and decorated with cellophane, ribbons, balloons, and bows. It's a tradition she hopes will continue forever.

Christmas is, by far, the number-one holiday for gift-basket giving. Individuals and corporations order them by the dozens. Friends, family, coworkers, and employees look forward to peeling back the cellophane closure to find a variety of gifts and treats in appreciation of support, friendship, or a job well done during the year. Personal and corporate gift baskets often include the same items—except, of course, when it comes to personal-care products and intimate apparel. While it's appropriate for friends to exchange perfumes and fragrances, corporations steer clear of buying these very personal items. They may, however, offer a gift certificate to a department store where the recipient can choose personal goods at his or her own discretion..

This holiday basket, created in a red sleigh, is fun and easy to make. It can be created in a traditional basket, or you can add dozens of extra items for one person or an entire family. Packing paper is added underneath the mixed white and gold shred. Floral foam was an option to elevate the products; however, foam would not look attractive in the small spaces on

The Christmas basket.

Cookies, dips, soups, and more create a festive celebration.

An open weave on the basket's side requires a clean attractive appearance.

the sleigh's sides. The container's construction creates a sturdy base to include everything for the holiday's festivities.

The wooden sleigh is solid red in color. It's a large and weighty container, especially when filled as you see here, so extra care is needed when you wrap the completed design. This basket includes spinach dip mix, French-onion-soup mix, fruity dip mix, chocolate-flavored Christmas cookies, flavored nut snacks, a specialty cake mix, and a large can of assorted teas and coffees disguised as a snowman. There are individuals who will receive your gift baskets that do not believe in Santa due to religious or cultural reasons. For that reason, the dip and cookies with a Santa image on the packaging are easily replaced by similar items with non-Santa graphics. The cake mix in front, packaged in the clear round container, may be appropriate for most people regardless of culture, as it states SEASON'S GREETINGS on the label rather than the word CHRISTMAS.

Designers often add a generous amount of embellishments in their Christmas designs. This one includes red and burgundy berry picks, pine twigs and cones, candy canes, and red berry foliage. Two sprays of golden onion grass are added, one on each side of the sleigh, to offset the greenery. Be very choosy when deciding how much foliage to add to your baskets. Some floral items cost as much as foods and gifts, which is why it's common to see full- and part-time designers buying their enhancements during sales events before and after the holidays. Swags are

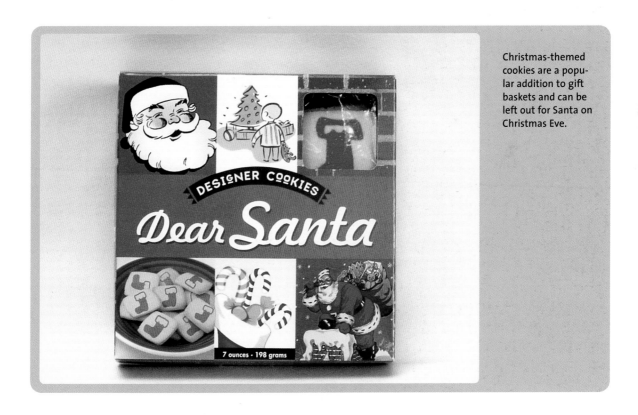

Christmas-themed cookies are a popular addition to gift baskets and can be left out for Santa on Christmas Eve.

another type of embellishment to consider. They're long, wired, and full of pretty holiday-themed pieces to drape around the basket's rim. A grapevine swag is shown with the Get-Well basket in chapter 7 (see page 78). Swags are found in craft stores, usually in the same area with picks and other decorative enhancements.

The sleigh's sides are woven in traditional basket-weaving fashion. Its small openings between the slats allow recipients to see the material used to elevate the products, but not by much. If this creates self-conscious doubt as you create your design, line the inner basket with tissue paper before inserting the packing paper. Red is a good color, as it complements the sleigh, but red's not the only choice. Select a color that's best for your design. Then you can continue creating your masterpiece with confidence.

One more thing I must bring to your attention is balance. A heavy gift basket, such as this sleigh, has a tendency to feel awkward when picked up if the products' weight distribution is off-center. For example, if you add a heavy bottle on one side, counterbalance it with a heavy item or a collection of lighter-weight items on the other side. This will ensure stability when shipping or handing the gift directly to the receiver.

Chocolate-flavored Christmas cookies are featured in this sleigh basket, but have you seen cookies with a stocking image stamped on top? Children are sure to enjoy leaving these and milk on a table in hopes that Santa will leave gifts under the tree.

Basket alternatives to the sleigh include a punch bowl, gift box, coffee or tea pot, ceramic gingerbread house, and large mug. An ice bucket was my client's favorite container. Ice buckets can be aluminized and sprayed in gold, green, or silver. Champagne, glasses, a

heart-shaped pillow, and a month's supply of bubble bath were another Christmas gift created for a husband to give to his spouse.

There are many options to add Christmas cheer to your baskets. As with a birthday basket and other arrangements, the chosen products will depend on the receiver's preferences. They may also depend on whether the person was naughty or nice!

Hanukkah

I was unfamiliar with making Hanukkah baskets until several clients requested gifts for customers who celebrate the tradition. Hanukkah, a religious event (the word is Hebrew for "dedication"), is celebrated for eight days and nights. It commemorates the victory over the Syrian armies in 165 B.C.E. One candle on the menorah is lit on each of the eight days. The Shamash, the highest candle, is used to light the others, and blessings are restated each night before the lighting.

Many of the companies from which I purchased products also sold kosher items (as evident by the kosher symbol on the package's back), and that made the selection easier as I filled my clients' orders. The basket size wasn't huge, nor was it required to be. Each had to show appreciation for the year's business. The baskets were mailed either to a small office or to the client's home and included enough items to share with a spouse or office staff.

As with creating a Kwanzaa basket (see page 111), I did some research to ensure that the color selection was appropriate. Blue and silver dominate the color scheme, so I chose products and supplies of those hues. The client was pleased with his customers' responses, and I was able to broaden my specialty designs to reflect a new group of baskets.

An open-weave basket is used for this Hanukkah design. The weave is particularly wide, and the blue tissue paper is visible between the openings. White tissue is also included. I added packing paper before topping the basket with gold and white shred. Blue shred was another option, but the gold and white mix makes a dynamic contrast against the tissue paper. This medium-sized basket pairs well with the items, which are tightly packed to create a stable and upright design.

The kosher products in this basket are fudge-filled walnut cookies, a small cake, orange thimble cookies, a ready-to-make pasta meal, vanilla pecan tea cookies, and an oval-shaped silver tray. The tray creates a deco-rative addition and can be used to serve the cakes and cookies within the basket. One silver star spray is placed on the right. A shorter, silver pick is an option in front, and silver tissue paper is a substitute for the blue and white tissue combination.

Menorah candles, dreidels, and children's books that explain the history of Hanukkah are other items that fit into this design. Latkes, gelt (chocolate coins), cheese blintzes, *sufganiyot* (jelly doughnuts), and other food items with the kosher stamp of approval can be incorporated within this mix to create an impressive arrangement. Such a basket must be hand-delivered rather than shipped, because most of these foods require immediate refrigeration. The only

The Hanukkah basket.

Kosher products of all kinds are a natural choice for Hanukkah baskets.

A silver serving tray positioned in back complements the color scheme and makes a lovely keepsake.

time it can be shipped is when the dry ingredients to make traditional Hanukkah foods are mailed.

Couples who are celebrating their first Hanukkah together may appreciate a basket that includes a menorah and candles. Such baskets need to be wide rather than tall and aren't more expensive than traditional baskets. Containers are another option. You may find corrugated boxes with Star of David symbols depicted on the front and back. Large, two-piece dreidels are capable of holding a collection of celebratory products. There are also companies that specialize in Hanukkah goods with a wide variety of items for adults and children—items that are perfect for gift basket inclusion.

If a basket isn't appropriate, tote bags are another handy item to create a Hanukkah present. A tote lined with a coordinating tissue and filled with a packing-paper foundation is the beginning of a thoughtful gift. My former insurance agent ordered such a bag with four kosher items including nuts and biscotti. She distributed the totes to more than a hundred clients, who were pleased that she showed appreciation for selecting her as their agent. Not all of these clients celebrated Hanukkah, but the products were universal to most taste buds. These gifts were very easy to create and took less time than designing a hundred baskets, although, of course, the latter would have been just as beautiful.

Kwanzaa

Kwanzaa is a nonreligious event that occurs from December 26 to January 1. It was created in 1966 by Dr. Maulana Karenga to celebrate African-American heritage. Kwanzaa is not an alternative to Christmas, and because it's not based on religion, people from all backgrounds are welcome to celebrate this occasion. The seven principles of Kwanzaa, known as the Nguzo Saba (a Swahili term that means "first fruits"), are recited each day, and the participants use the principles to reflect on their family, community, and heritage.

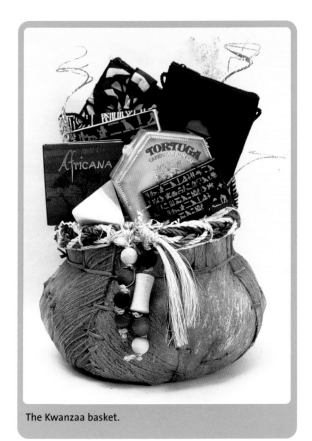

The Kwanzaa basket.

A Kwanzaa basket is based on items with an African or Caribbean background. You'll find an abundance of products that contain African-based colors and symbols available, some of which are shown in this Kwanzaa basket. The vessel is African in origin and expresses the theme of this wonderful design. It's made from three pieces of cloth sewn together with thin leather cord on the sides and bottom. A tricolored braided rope is secured around the basket's rim. Two strands of beads dangle in front, or the beads can be positioned on the side or back.

The contents include a rum cake, a pyramid-shaped paperweight, a book containing African proverbs, a business-card holder and notebook with hieroglyphics stamped on the front and back covers, four coasters made from African material, a cosmetics-purse set made with African material, and a small black pocketbook with a patch shaped to resemble the African continent sewn in the middle.

The products are elevated with packing paper on the basket's inside, topped with beige-colored shred, which is pushed down slightly so that the braid around the basket remains visible. Black, gold, brown, beige, green, and red are the colors that unite this theme. Glue dots are used to anchor the products together. Notice the glue dot placement between the business-card holder and rum-cake package. There aren't many embellishments within this design, but few are needed. Ting-ting and wild grass are added in back for height.

Alternate containers include boxes in colors of black, red, green, or gold. General baskets are also useful; the products will create the Kwanzaa theme. Figurines, pyramid-shaped candies or chocolates, home decor items (table runners, napkins, cloths, and the

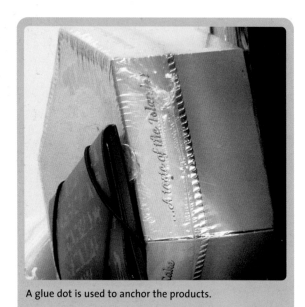

A glue dot is used to anchor the products.

Museum shops are a good source for Kwanzaa-themed products.

like), adult and children's books, CDs of African music, and African coffee are Kwanzaa basket items found in stores. Museums and specialty shops are good places to find items that are African-based. The notebook and business-card holder were made especially for the Brooklyn (New York) Museum, a place where many Egyptian antiquities are on permanent display.

It used to be difficult to find Kwanzaa products that were affordable while still reflecting tradition. Now that many cultural traditions are embraced within the United States and abroad, it's become easier to find items that denote the African experience.

Wholesalers make food and gift items for various cultures, which can be found in local stores around the country.

Several designers specialize in Kwanzaa baskets, especially in areas where there's a large concentration of African-American residents. Their clients look forward to the celebration and present gifts when traveling or to each person within a family. One designer located in the Midwest creates Kwanzaa baskets using a plain white box and mudcloth or kente fabric. She covers the box with the fabric and uses glue to secure it in place. It's an inexpensive method that creates a stunning design, which sells briskly at year's end.

You may not have a need to make Kwanzaa baskets, but you will become more aware of the products that create this celebratory theme when you are looking for items for all-occasion baskets.

10 Think Out of the Basket

Alternative Containers Challenge Your Creativity

Baskets will always be the main vessel for our gifts, but other types of containers have become just as popular in recent years. People love receiving a container they can reuse in a foyer, bedroom, dining area, or other location in or out of the home. Flowerpots, vases, wagons, teacups, mugs, and boxes are examples of nonbasket containers that can be used to design packages.

My business was built around containers. I used rocking chairs for retirement gifts, wagons for new babies, upturned umbrellas for bridal showers, and flowerpots for gardeners. Each gift sold quickly because the buyer loved the fact that recipients would enjoy seeing the container in their homes or offices. Of course, baskets can be used more than once, too, but a container seems to add its own brand of excitement.

In September 1994 I wanted to appear on The Food Network, so I sent a producer a teacup and saucer lined with fruit-filled cookies freshly baked by my sister, Cassandra. Each cookie was wrapped and skewered to resemble a lollipop. The entire design was closed in cellophane, and I drove to the show's studio on Sixth Avenue in New York to present it along with printed materials about my company.

The producer called an hour after I delivered the design. He was interested in having me as a guest on a show but wasn't able to find time. Another producer saw my information, and I appeared on another show on December 26, 1994. The audience was treated to New Year's gifts designed in top hats, briefcases, silver-plated trays, and wine buckets. That three-minute appearance exposed my containered gifts to more than twenty-two million viewers worldwide. I received calls from people who not only wanted more

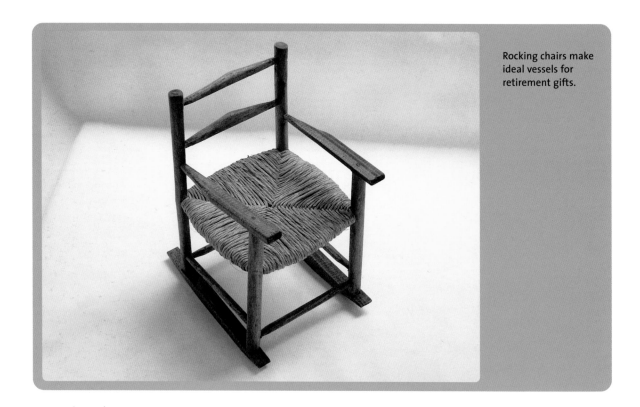

Rocking chairs make ideal vessels for retirement gifts.

information but also from those who ordered on the spot. It was an extraordinary experience that proved how much people adore containers.

Fruit-Decorated Box

Boxes create magnificent gifts. They're available in many shapes and used for various purposes. Some are specifically for hats, and others hold jewelry, clothing, or shoes. Interior designers choose nested boxes to embellish living-space corners. You'll see these boxes stacked atop each other in sets of three, four, or five, all in the same pattern. They're usually square in shape, but some are oval.

A box is rigid enough to hold anything. It will support an item as light as a pen or as heavy as a bottle of cider. The square box used here (see page 115), decorated in apples, pears, cherries, lemons, and grapes, is great for celebrating birthdays, wishing good luck, saying thank-you, offering as a house-warming gift, and more. It's covered in paper rather than fabric. The finish contains a slightly raised pattern. The vertical perforations are also visible if you look closely at the box and lid.

Inside this box are Bavarian-style pretzels, key lime mustard, key-lime-flavored cookies, and a cup and saucer. A beverage isn't always required because a cup is included. Perhaps the person who will receive this gift has broken a favorite saucer set, and this one is a replacement. Others may prefer a specific blend of coffee or tea to which you have no access. If a design

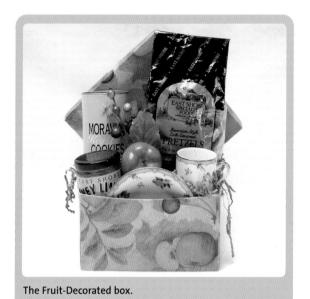

The Fruit-Decorated box.

The key-lime-flavored treats and fruit-covered cup and saucer continue the fruit theme.

has no room for a beverage, but you'd still like to include one, do so in the cup.

Key-lime-flavored products may remind the recipient of a vacation to a southern state or perhaps bring back childhood memories. If key lime isn't the preferred flavor, these products can be swapped for another such as tangerine, apricot, lemon, or strawberry. A pancake mix and syrup, scones, a plush toy, or stationery are suggested alternatives.

What makes this arrangement better for a woman than a man is the teacup with saucer. Some men wouldn't mind receiving such a decorative product, but others would prefer a set in solid green or burgundy. Aside from that, it's a wonderful gift anyone would love to receive.

The box's lid creates a faux back wall. It could have been placed on the bottom to hold the box, but using the lid as a decorative "wall" is the better option. To create this look, insert the lid so that one corner peaks upward at the midpoint. The pattern should face forward. Packing paper and shred are the cushion, and both are added before or after the lid enters the box. There's no need to fill the open lid facing the back with shred or an embellishment.

When all the products are in place, a small apple and berry pick are inserted. The pretzel's bag is folded down by approximately $1/4$ inch at the top and taped in place. Glue dots are another way to shorten a package's height.

Boxes are very easy to close within cellophane, a basket bag, or shrink wrap. Use the cellophane-closing technique described in chapter 6 as a guide (see page 46). The bottom corners create ninety-degree angles that keep the closure material smooth

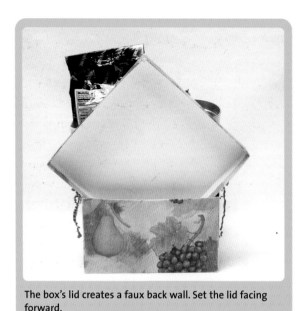
The box's lid creates a faux back wall. Set the lid facing forward.

Thank-You Box

Here's a box with lots of character. The design offers universal appeal by expressing thanks in several languages. This is one of the first boxes I used to create a gift ordered by a principal for his staff. All had experienced a disconcerting school year due to huge changes in personnel, including the principal's job. He asked me to make one gift for each of his twenty-five teachers and six office staff members. Everyone received the Thank-You box, customized according to each person's age and lifestyle. Making thirty-one different designs wasn't as difficult as it sounds. Some individuals received the same type of popcorn or cookies, but one staffer played golf, and another loved word puzzles. The differences made each container shine, and so did the recipients when they received the gifts.

The box's solid construction holds products sturdily and won't collapse during transit. Unlike similarly made smaller boxes with a straight brim, as shown throughout this chapter, this container's upper edge is notched in the front and back. Paper is the preferred filler for this box; you'd simply need too many foam bricks to elevate the products. Beige or vanilla-colored shred is too bland for this pretty container. Red was chosen, but blue, green, or yellow would be just as vivid.

It's easy to read the contents' labels except for one—the scone mix. Caramel popcorn, spice cookies, the baking mix, a wine-jelly assortment, roasted-red-pepper jam, and New York–style cheesecake fill the box. A Realtor would adore this type of design to present to a new homeowner. A friend who's been supportive through a crisis is another deserving

and tight on all sides. There's no need to fold gaps to be taped underneath—the corner edges ensure a clean presentation.

You can find similar boxes at card stores, boutique shops, and chain stores such as Target and Wal-Mart. Don't be surprised if office suppliers offer boxes on their clearance table after the holidays. Chocolates, cookies, candies, and a variety of containers are the first items to go on sale after December 25. Review the prices, and decide if such goods are worth buying.

When the recipient removes all of the products, the decorated box becomes a handy reusable container. A man can use the box to organize his favorite colognes or bathroom toiletries. A woman might arrange teas and accessories (tea strainer, spoons, cubed sugar, honey sticks, what have you) under the lid. Potpourri, nail-care items, and plush animals are other items that might be stored in the empty box.

recipient. It's also a great way for newlyweds to express their appreciation to both sets of parents. This gift or a smaller version containing three or four items may be the right size for a neighbor who retrieves the mail and newspaper while you're on vacation. There's someone in your life who deserves this gift.

Decorative fans are the only enhancement added to the design. They serve as a striking back-drop while supporting the three products in back. Other embellishments are acceptable, but there are times when less is better. The ribbon tied around the box of assorted wine jellies is a pretty and deco-rative touch. Many manufacturers embellish their products in this manner, and so can you. It's a way to add class to the entire design by using just one piece of ribbon.

This design is beautiful because of its simplicity. There are no stacking or positioning dilemmas; three products are placed next to each other in two rows. Finding products that theme well together and fit within a container's width isn't an easy task. As you become accustomed to gift-basket making, however, you'll develop a sense for selecting products that cre-ate beautiful arrangements in a fair amount of time. A gift basket that takes you forty-five minutes the first time will take thirty minutes the next and fifteen minutes thereafter.

The Thank-You box.

This box is sturdy enough to hold hefty products with ease.

Decorative fans placed in back are the only embellishment this design needs.

As with the fruit box, you'll find any of the popular cellophane closures to be a satisfactory choice. Basket bags are made solely to fit this box. If you'll be shipping the gift out of town, you might consider using a two-pronged wrapping solution of shrink wrap first, then a soft cellophane covering.

Pet treats are a thoughtful addition in a thank-you basket if the receiver owns a four-legged friend. One designer bought a set of bones in Styrofoam packaging that resembled supermarket-style meat. It was closed in plastic wrap and tied with a pretty bow. She added it to her customer's basket after finding out that the recipient owned a dog. The receiver was thrilled because the prized pooch was acknowledged.

Thanksgiving Box

Giving thanks is not only practiced at home but also shared when invited to another person's house. Or perhaps you're someone who distributes Thanksgiving gifts rather than baskets for Christmas. Small, printed boxes make a friendly substitute for a basket. They allow men and women to present or receive gifts that don't leave the impression of going to Grandma's house.

The container shown here is a breeze to style. Designers love this sturdy paper box because it stores flat when not in use and sets up easily by twisting the bottom connectors into place. The large box shown in the Thank-You design is just as simple to store (see page 117). The Thanksgiving box holds four to five products, depending on size, and wraps easily within cellophane or a custom-sized basket bag. One floral foam brick fits perfectly in the bottom if skewers are preferred to anchor each product. Packing paper secures each item just as well, and that's the method used here. Orange-colored shred matches the colors on the box. If the person who's to receive this doesn't celebrate Thanksgiving, there's also a box designed with fall leaves, an appropriate choice for individuals from other cultures.

What Thanksgiving hostess wouldn't appreciate receiving a selection of items that she can relax and enjoy or prepare before joining the mad shopping rush on Friday? Seasoned nuts and snack crackers are quick to eat, while pancake mix and apricot syrup create a bountiful breakfast for a weekend morning. Another option, as shown in many designs in this book, is to either fill the hostess gift with all open-and-eat snacks or different types of mixes, especially if you know that the hostess loves to cook. Cookie and cake mixes, along with a selection of cookie cutters, fit perfectly in this box. A magnetic or cubed notepad, small wall plaque, meat rub and seasonings, and unscented candles are other options for this package.

This gift box is lined with goldenrod tissue, while floral enhancements and a gold berry pick add flair around the products. Adding tissue can be a challenge because the outcome is always abstract. Use craft scissors or pinking shears to cut and shape the

This box stores flat when not in use . . .

. . . then sets up easily, ready to be filled.

The Thanksgiving box.

Packing paper is used to fill the box, although floral foam would work just as well.

tissue's edges, or let the natural shaping stay as is. In either case, your Thanksgiving gift will be a thoughtful memento, as it expresses gratitude toward a friend, loved one, or a person you've just met.

Black-and-White-Striped Box

When I see black and white, I think of fashion. No matter what colors are in vogue, basic black and white will always be on the runway. Such classic colors are the focus for this boxed gift. The Thanksgiving box features a holiday design using many colors, but boxes can present a timeless appearance. The black-and-white stripes might also be viewed as a corporate look—something you'd give to, say, an executive. A second marriage, college graduation, or other types of personal achievement are also appropriate occasions for this style.

Shred in shades of purple, burgundy, or pink presents a striking contrast to this box design, as well as products with packaging that highlights similar colors. This gift and its contents focus on the black-and-white format. Packing paper fills the bottom, topped with mixed white and gold shred. Peanut brittle, orange-walnut cookies, double fudge cookies, chocolate dipping sauce, and a plastic cone filled with ice cream toppings create a delicious assortment that's great for any occasion.

Friends often ask me for men's gifts ideas, and I suggest this type of design. Cattails can replace the flowered pick on the left, or enhancements can be

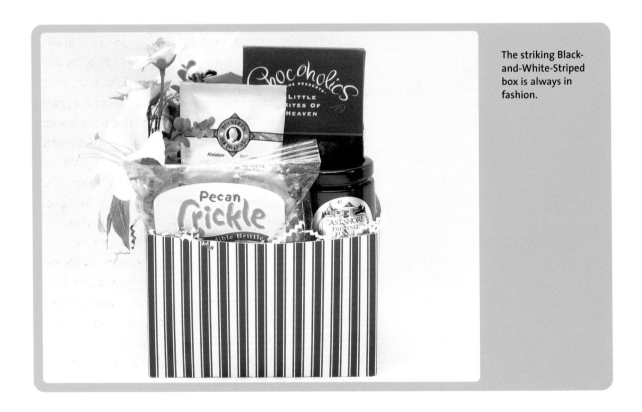

The striking Black-and-White-Striped box is always in fashion.

Printed cellophane and a mesh bow add the finishing touches.

used to close this basket, and the gold mesh bow adds elegance.

A small basket is just as simple to use for this design, but it's great to see alternatives to using traditional vessels. All of us want to show our creativity when giving gifts, whether that means finding a product with exotic flavoring or a container that's new and unique. Blending wonderful gifts with unique styling is what makes your creations so appealing to all who receive them.

Always look for beautiful baskets and unique containers that keep your design style fresh and inspiring. Consider anything with an open middle as the start of your masterpiece.

Chocoholic Design

Are you a person who craves at least one piece of chocolate every day? Join the club. Chemists tell us that this sweet treat alters a person's mood for the better, but instead of being scientific, why not make a chocoholic basket and let the recipient be the judge?

Here's the ultimate chocoholic's delight, a selection of items that are either made from chocolate, include chocolate, or are ready for dipping into chocolate. You're no doubt familiar with some of the items, but others will be a pleasant surprise. Chocolate pasta, raspberry dessert topping, seasoned pretzels, dipping fudge, tranquility chocolate onfections, a one-minute microwavable chocolate cake, chocolate squares from Brussels, crème de mint chocolate cocoa, and chocolate-raspberry coffee bring you as close to chocolate heaven as you can imagine.

A striking hat box in a half-moon shape and made with white brocade material creates a beautiful

omitted entirely. It's a simple, couch-potato-type box of treats to enjoy while watching a favorite television show or rented movie.

The jar of dipping fudge is weighty and initially sank down into the box so that its label was covered. Extra packing paper was added to the space, and shred was placed on top before repositioning the fudge. It now sits tall without wobbling so that the recipient will see the label. This was easy to do, especially because raising the jar didn't affect the fudge cookies' box. The same technique was shown in chapter 4 to elevate jam (see page 34). Cellophane is

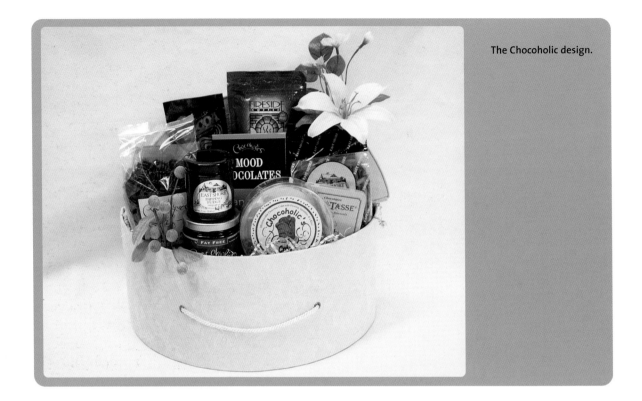

appearance for the products. It's accented with a white rope cord inserted into the box through two grommets. The box and lid are lined in black velvet. One floral foam brick is used in back, and packing paper lines the box's front curve and upper portion. Pink-colored shred cushions the products. Two picks in pink shades complement the shred. Glue dots stabilize the dipping fudge atop the raspberry sauce.

The box's lid is inserted into the back at an angle. It's the only way that the lid will fit properly to give the design height; placing the lid under the box would be an uncreative decision. One edge is pushed down into the box, while the other sits on top. You can see the lid's black velvet interior from the back view.

The chocolate pasta and raspberry topping are paired for eating together, although it's not mandatory. This pasta, made in spiral curl shapes, is a dessert rather than dinner. It's cooked in the traditional way, then cooled and drizzled with the sauce. Consider this an exotic treat for someone who's tasted just about everything or a sensual product that completes a Valentine's Day basket. Chocolate lovers who enjoy the combined taste of sweet and salty will dip the pretzels into the fudge sauce.

Your favorite chocoholic will love the microwavable cake, packaged with frosting, sprinkles, a candle,

A white brocade hat box sets off this assortment of chocolate goodies.

Insert the box's black-velvet-lined lid into the back with one end peeking out.

A rear view reveals the elegance of this half-moon shaped container.

and a balloon. It's mixed with water in the clear, round container in which it's packaged. After microwaving it for one minute, spread the frosting, add sprinkles, light the candle (after placing it in the cake), and blow up the balloon for a personal chocoholics party. These cakes are available in many themes such as cheer up, happy birthday, and teacher and are extremely popular in gift baskets.

Chocolate bars, chocolate snack cakes, truffles, four-piece candy boxes, chocolate bath products (chocolate items for the skin), Oreos, chocolate biscotti, and chocolate cookies are considerations for your custom design. A mix of chocolate snacks from the supermarket and chocolate goodies from upscale stores creates a balanced collection of treats to devour.

One West Coast company makes square and heart-shaped chocolate boxes—that is, the actual box

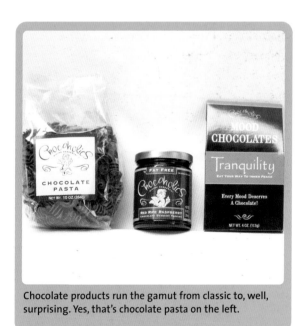

Chocolate products run the gamut from classic to, well, surprising. Yes, that's chocolate pasta on the left.

is made of chocolate. Each shape is filled with round chocolate confections and coffee beans and sealed on top with a chocolate lid that sits within a molded lip. After eating the contents, the box is broken apart and eaten bit by bit. I gave my bank's manager the square-shaped box for her wedding anniversary. She called to thank me and ordered twelve boxes for clients who had recently made substantial deposits. How's that for chocolate overload?

If you live with chocoholics, be sure to tuck this design out of sight until time for delivery. That's the only way to keep you from returning to the store to buy items that mysteriously disappear.

More Out-of-the-Basket Designs

Totes, Trunks, Towers, and More

Baskets and boxes are just the beginning. There are many other items—some right in your own basement, attic, or garage—that can serve as beautiful containers. Here's a look at a few additional nonbasket containers that can be used to create your next gift basket masterpiece.

Tote Bag

Bags make a fashion statement. Many are still available in solid colors, but others are splashed with multiple hues, trimmed with lace, or adorned with beads. People love bags, so manufacturers create new styles to keep these items selling briskly in card, party, and other small shops.

Bags aren't as fragile as they appear. At first glance this paper-based item might seem unable to support a collection of products. However, the pictured bag in a burgundy fleur-de-lis pattern is a willing container for four average-weight products. Packing paper fills the bottom portion to create a rigid foundation, yet not so tightly as to distort the bag's shape. Very little shred is added before product insertion. You can place enough shred on the inside to cascade above the edge, but for this example, that would conceal the products' names.

This design serves to show gratitude. It can be presented at the door of a person who's invited you to a party, in appreciation for kindness when none was expected, or for watching a residence while the owner was away. The secondary reason for this gift is instant gratification. Cheese straws, caramelized popcorn, and thimble cookies are ready to be opened and eaten immediately. Round coasters printed with trivia questions and answers are the fourth item. For this gift, recipients must provide their own beverage and

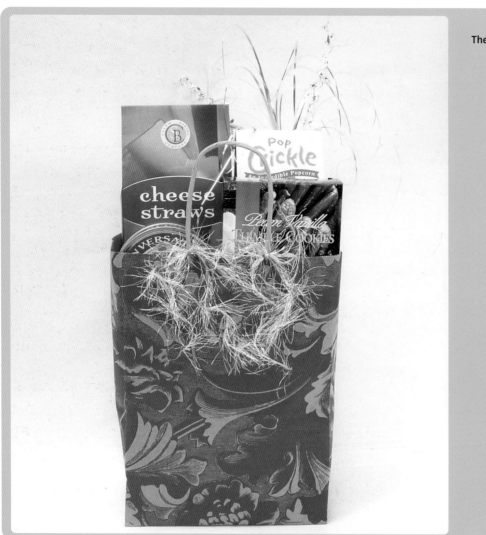

cups, but after reviewing the contents, I doubt that they'll mind.

Years ago designers cut cardboard to fit along the bag's four sides. Paper was added, followed by products. This gift is so simple to make that designers no longer waste time cutting cardboard. The tote won't fall as long as the products are of equal weight distributed on all sides.

The silver strand enhancement tied to the handles is called eyelash ribbon. It's wired and easy to curl, making a more elegant appearance than regular curling ribbon. If your local craft store doesn't sell eyelash ribbon, don't let that stop you from adding curling ribbon. Star spray is shown at the back.

Closing a bag is similar to closing a square container. The edges are at 90-degree angles, which

Use packing paper to fill the bag and create a rigid foundation.

Add just a bit of shred in the bag.

An assortment of interesting products makes the Tote bag a lovely gesture of thanks.

makes closure simple. After folding the bag or cellophane closed, top it with a bow. Add star spray above the cellophane fan for a little extra pizzazz.

I've used tote bags to combine popcorn, bowls, and napkins for post office clerks at the locations I visit most. During the country's anthrax scare in 2001, I knew that the postal workers felt vulnerable. The extra bags of popcorn in my inventory were leftovers from a gift-basket-design class concluded a month earlier. First, I lined the totes with tissue paper. Then I placed napkins in the bag, followed by Styrofoam dessert bowls. This allowed the two bags of popcorn, one caramel and one butter, to sit tall, and everyone

Patterned cello and a burgundy bow complete this look.

could see the contents. Because the workers knew me, they were grateful to enjoy a snack from someone they trusted. Spreading a little joy was rewarding, and it helped some of our most dedicated workers get on with their lives.

Tote bags are available in many sizes and shapes. Some resemble mugs, cups and saucers, and brief-cases. Others are triangular in shape, are studded with grommets, or contain rope handles rather than twisted paper. Bags are decorated with animals, insects, fruits, or flowers. Their versatility allows us to create beautiful gifts or store the bags flat until a use presents itself. And the affordable price will inspire you to create terrific Tote bag designs.

Trunk

Beautiful containers such as this trunk are the type of object that many long to receive. You'll see shoppers pick them up and caress them in those large linen stores selling everything from candles to bedding. Then they put the trunks down again when they spot the price tag! Trunks can be quite expensive, no matter what the size. They're frequently used in home decor, which serves to support the outrageous cost.

This sample is a tabletop model, slim yet large enough to hold numerous items. Its rectangular shape is decorated in a sturdy, beige cloth covered in wine bottle shapes, wine-associated names, and grapes. The interior is beige in color and smooth to

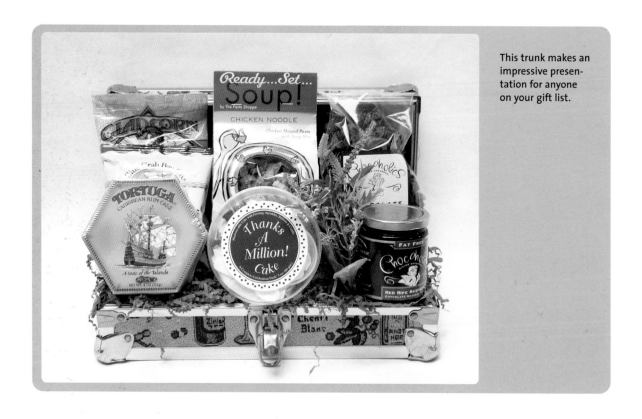

This trunk makes an impressive presentation for anyone on your gift list.

the touch. A lock is fastened to the front. The trunk's corners are protected with metal bumpers secured with studs, but don't let that fool you into thinking it can't be dented. I've traveled with this trunk to conduct gift-basket seminars and packed it in bubble wrap in my luggage. It now has a permanent airline souvenir—a small impression within the gold plating.

You can choose to cut floral foam to fit the trunk's bottom or add two sheets of packing paper to fill the interior before adding shred. Green-colored shred was chosen because it highlights the green colors within the trunk's design. Many products fit into this container. Included are corn snacks, seasoned nuts, rum cake, chicken noodle soup, Thanks a Million cake, chocolate pasta, and raspberry dessert topping. One pick was added in the opening between the cake and dessert sauce.

The cake's theme, Thanks a Million, dictates the reason for this gift. It's a special design that's used to impress the receiver. I created several trunk designs for an executive vice president of a pharmaceutical firm. He asked that each gift be hand-delivered to the homes and temporary apartments of job candidates who were recommended by high-level contacts. An accountant also asked for such a gift to be delivered to her best client.

You may not work with high-powered clients, but you will find reasons to create trunk gift designs. For example, I have a friend who loves scuba diving, and I could think of no better container for her birthday than a trunk. I chose one in a square shape and a design similar to the one shown on this page. Then I transformed the empty vessel into a sunken treasure masterpiece. She screamed with delight as she opened the lid to see two handfuls of coins and other

This tabletop trunk is sturdy, beautiful, and reusable.

Both floral foam and packing paper make appropriate trunk fillers.

With their spacious interiors, trunks can hold a great many gifts.

gold-wrapped chocolates, several white-chocolate starfish, a pair of goggles, a spyglass, a fantasy pirate's map, an eye patch, Mardi Gras–type necklaces, and miniature sunken ships (the type used in fish tanks). Can you think of a similar design that someone will love receiving?

Decorative trunks are found in a variety of colors and styles. Many times you'll find them at yard sales and other low-cost events where someone else's trash becomes your newfound treasure.

Gourmet Tower

Up to now you've seen each container filled from the inside. The vessel is packed with floral foam or paper, and products are mounted in place surrounded by coordinating embellishments. But not every container has to be filled on the inside. Why not flip a container, using the outside bottom as a base to build a gift upward in pyramid style? That's what's done with this beautiful laminated box with cutout handles on each side.

The gold-swirled design on an off-white background reflects a celebration or cheerful scene. It's a great container for a basic design, but when you flip it over, the pattern becomes a focal point and gets the attention it deserves. This technique is part of the "thinking out of the box" routine that designers are faced with every day when asked to create something different. Items that would normally be added on the inside are stacked atop each other, and the gift is

This swirl-pattern box makes a lovely container—but you can also flip it upside down and use it as a base for a tower creation.

enclosed in cellophane and topped with a dazzling bow. What person wouldn't love to receive a tower of treats?

A rum cake is the first and widest item, sitting directly on the box. Its goldenrod packaging makes a beautiful contrast to the box. Next is a can of spicy snack mix. The can's sky-blue label works for this towering gift because there's a hint of blue on the rum cake package. Last is a can of lemon cookies. Its label is also lemon, which matches the border around the rum cake's box. Each product's package is smaller than the one just below. That's a necessity to create this gift. Color matching, though mentioned here, isn't as important.

Boxes, bags, and tins can be of differing shapes, as long as each sits evenly atop the rest. The taller the gift, the more valuable it's perceived as being. Don't, however, stack a design to rival the Empire State Building! Three or four items are best. If you create anything taller, the gift might become unmanageable as you attempt to close it within cellophane or shrink wrap. Unfortunately, no basket bag is tall enough to enclose this design.

Place at least two glue dots between the top and bottom of each product. This includes the container and the rum cake just above it. The area around the bottom of each product doesn't have to stay bare. Some designers twist garland around each product's base, and some leave it clean. Before wrapping the design, you may consider adding shred on the container, directly around the first product.

Have your bow ready before closing the design. A true designer won't measure, cut, and apply cellophane only to release a perfect wrap to make a bow. Cut the cellophane so that a 3- to 5-inch width

To create a tower, look for gifts in graduating sizes: large, small, smaller.

Stack the products skyscraper-style.

Add two or more glue dots between the products.

The completed Gourmet Tower.

completely out of the design. If that were the case here, the rum cake would serve as the base.

My Get-Well gifts feature a square, 500-piece puzzle box as the base, with other busy-hands items decreasing in size stacked atop. The last item is usually a cup and saucer with a small package of cookies and the recipient's favorite beverage in the cup. Stacking is an easy process. The main drawback is finding items that both stack together and match the receiver's preferences. Still, given all the products available to you, it will not be difficult to strike a balance between the two.

Practice making your first tower gift with a maximum of three items, including the container if you choose to add one. You may love the design so much that you'll decide to keep it instead of giving it away.

Latte Tower

Small cups and saucers aren't the only containers that work well inside baskets or as stand-alone gifts. Many designers incorporate oversized cup sets within tower gifts or as a single gift option for a person who requires extra pizzazz as part of the presentation. Latte is associated with larger cups. Originating in France, it's a drink made with espresso and steamed milk and served in an oversized cup.

The sample gift depicted here is another tower option. It combines a latte cup and saucer, a tin container of dipping pretzels and mustard, key lime straw snacks, cappuccino, and two flavored spoons. You can turn the saucer upside down to create a base, as done here, or leave the saucer so that the edges are pointing upward. Either method works, because the saucer is solid green on both sides. The black-and-white-checked tin sits atop the saucer and is easy to position.

remains on each side. That will ensure that there's enough room for proper closure. Seal the cellophane with tape on either side, and close it on top with a bow. Extra curling ribbon looks great, or you can add long tails to the bow to drape into place on each side of the tower. Glue dots help to position the wavy ribbon.

The same design can be created using a thin flat base such as an inverted silver tray (any size, with or without handles), a tray table or serving tray, or a cutting board. Another option is to anchor your tower of gifts with a gift or food product, leaving a tray or box

The Latte Tower design.

A rear view of the Latte Tower's top, with a favorite beverage tucked in back.

Mardi Gras beads make a colorful addition, if you like, for a female recipient.

A regular-sized cup would work above the tin, but this oversized cup adds balance to the entire design. The box of key lime straws is inserted first into the cup. White and gold-colored shred is tucked in the spaces between the cup and box. Flavored spoons are inserted on the left, followed by a package of cappuccino at the back and small pick on the right. Mardi Gras–type beads add interest around the cup but aren't needed if you can't find a source for them. In addition, you might want to skip them if a man is to receive this gift.

As with the tall tower design, glue dots are secured between the cup, saucer, and tin. The key lime straw box is tall, eliminating the need for packing paper or floral foam within the cup. Close this design in cellophane or shrink wrap. Your bow choice will depend on the person to receive this design. A green or black-and-white bow fits for a man or woman. In addition, a combination yellow-and-green bow works for a woman.

More Out-of-the-Basket Designs

This is a typical all-occasion gift that's simple to make. The tin adds height, but don't overlook other items. For instance, a boxed cake, a container of cookies, or a tin of chocolates each make wonderful substitutes. Latte cups are available in many colors. They are found in supermarkets and specialty stores and sometimes at discounters. I've seen these cup combinations for a low as $3—a terrific price that rivals what some wholesalers charge their retail customers.

Keep this gift in mind whenever you want to make a presentation that towers above all others.

Cup and Saucer

A card-store owner asked me to come to her store to develop ideas to sell her cups and saucers. She had recently moved twenty-five sets to the clearance area, and they still weren't selling. It was late April, a great time to think about Mother's Day gifts. So I turned these beautifully designed sets decorated with pink and yellow rosebuds into gifts for moms.

Hard candies available in the store were gathered in handfuls and wrapped in cellophane closed with one string of curling ribbon. The candies were inserted into the cups. All twenty-five cups and saucers were wrapped in cellophane and topped with a small bow. The store owner positioned the newly packaged gifts around the checkout counter. Within three days everything was sold, and the store owner was surprised at how simple packaging turned teacups and saucers into an instant, full-priced success.

We often pass cup and saucer sets in clearance areas and at flea markets, never seeing the potential to make a thoughtful gift for an aunt, grandmother, or longtime friend. These sets are extremely easy to turn

The Cup-and-Saucer design.

into gift items. You can use snacks, candies, small gifts, and beverages to create a beautiful product in a matter of minutes.

In the design shown above, glue dots are used to anchor the cup and saucer together. Tissue paper lines the back of the cup. A small piece of floral foam is covered with tissue paper and inserted into the cup. Orange-colored shred is tucked into the cup and around the foam. Skewers are added to the back of the chocoholic's cake, cocoa mix, and chocolate-turtle-flavored coffee. This anchoring method is discussed in chapter 4 (see page 36). Each product is

These chocolate lover's gifts are supported in the cup with skewers. Any number of treats can be substituted.

rim such as shown in the mug design (see page 136). At this point it will be difficult to resist picking up every cup-and-saucer set sold at yard sales. But try not to buy them all unless you're selling them to a retailer who's looking for outside creativity.

Mugs

Who among us doesn't have assorted mugs in our home waiting to be filled with coffee, tea, flavored spoons, cookies, and other small goodies? Mugs are incredibly easy to design. This no-fuss container makes a perfect thank-you, welcome, or appreciation gift. The main consideration is finding items tall enough to fit both inside and above the rim, or adding attractive items that fit horizontally across the rim. Two mugs are shown here (see pages 136 and 138) to depict both design types.

The white mug is personalized with the name GENESIS. Such mugs are available in variety stores and are the basis for creating a customized gift specifically for birthdays and thank-yous. Red-colored shred fills the mug and stabilizes two extra items. Flavored sugar, the front product, is placed in the mug. A Post-it notepad and small tin of chocolates sit horizontally across the mug. Glue dots are used between each product as support. A package of cappuccino, which is tall enough to extend into the mug, is added behind the chocolates. An iced-tea spoon peeks above the cappuccino. Two picks and two pieces of ting-ting are added to the back, and the design is complete.

Mugs are often the gift of choice for supervisors who buy Administrative Professionals Day gifts for the office support staff team. Cookies, coffee, and flowers are bundled together. A small pick stating HAPPY ADMINISTRATIVE PROFESSIONALS DAY, which looks similar to

added to the cup, starting from the back. When the items are stabilized, place star spray at the back. A flavored spoon fills a slightly open space on the right. Small basket bags will create a snug fit for this set, or you can choose cellophane.

Cups and saucers create a favorite basketless design that takes about five minutes to complete from start to finish. The set's pattern reflects the recipient's tastes, and so do the contents. Cookies, biscotti, chocolates, jelly beans, tea, crackers, nuts, and candies are some of the options that fit into this petite pair. Individually wrapped hard candies can be placed on the saucer around the cup's bottom. These candies don't need anchoring. Each can move freely in the small space between the cup and cellophane.

Floral foam and skewers aren't requirements when working with a cup and saucer. Shred can be tucked between tall, slim items that extend above the

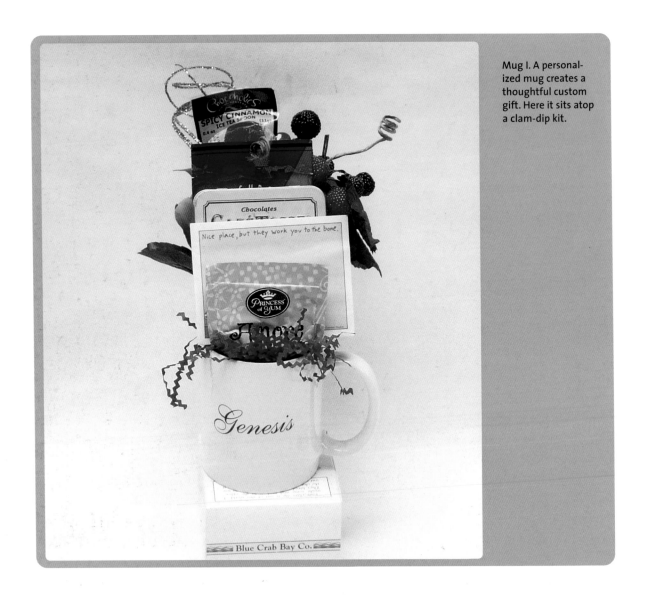

the HAPPY NEW YEAR's pick in chapter 9 (see page 96), is placed in front before wrapping.

Not all products will sit as steadily as the chocolates and notepad. Each is wide enough to fit across the mug's rim, and the extra support provided by the cappuccino, flavored coffee, and glue dots ensures that these products won't move before closing the gift in a basket bag or cellophane.

Consider placing an item directly below the mug. The square clam-dip kit package shown under the white mug is slightly larger and fits perfectly. Designers often add something special in this man-

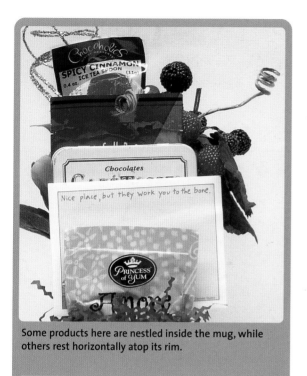

Some products here are nestled inside the mug, while others rest horizontally atop its rim.

Picks and ting-ting at the back complete the design.

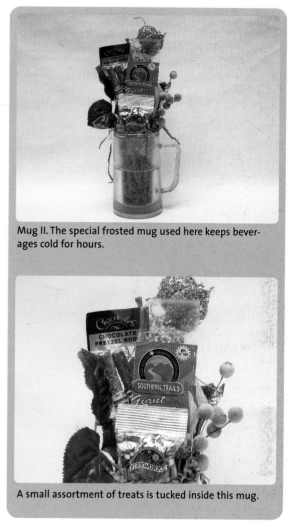

Mug II. The special frosted mug used here keeps beverages cold for hours.

A small assortment of treats is tucked inside this mug.

ner when a client requests a unique product that is too large to fit within the mug. Glue dots secure the two products together.

This mug is personalized, but your selection may not be. A cup, as used in the previous Cup-and-Saucer design, makes a terrific gift, as does any of the assortment of unused mugs in your kitchen cabinets, basement, or attic.

Mugs are available in all shapes and sizes, including the frosted mug shown in the second design. Distilled water is trapped within this mug's circular wall.

It's placed in the freezer so that the water freezes and keeps a beverage cold for hours. All the products in this design are contained within the mug. Green shred can be seen through the mug's transparent design. The shortest item, microwave popcorn, is in front. A beef stick is in the middle, and two chocolate-covered pretzel rods are in back.

Two embellishments are added. You don't, however, need a variety of picks for each mug. Some designs look stunning without extra flowers and curls. Look at your finished mug before adding to the cost with embellishments.

The frosted mug is wrapped with cellophane. Its sides are closed in the triangular format. A bow made from metallic chenille ribbon and enhanced with a flower pick brightens the look. The metallic chenille is wired, which makes curling and shaping the bow's loops and ends a snap.

You can add embellishments after the gift is wrapped. Here, a bow and flower add cheer.

PART 03

Beyond the Basics

12 Quick Fixes

Don't Get Mad, Get Creative!

Gift baskets and nonbasket designs provide a wide variety of options for all-occasion gift giving. You've learned new ways to create baskets, satisfied your curiosity about how designs are prepared, and seen many options to build gifts when baskets aren't available or needed.

When you visit a store and see beautiful gift baskets on shelves and pedestals, you're looking at the finished product. There's no indication of the problems that may have occurred during construction. All types of design problems arise for beginners and experts alike. Most situations have easy solutions, and others are so severe that you must start again.

In chapter 3 you learned about cutting floral foam and the consequences of cutting the foam too short. However, adding U-shaped pins between two bricks adds to the length, thereby solving the short-brick problem. Chapter 6 explained how to use a pick to mask a hole caused by excess heat on shrink wrap. What happens if you cut your cellophane so short that the height above the design looks stubby? Can it be fixed, or is it better to discard the cello? This chapter provides solutions for this and other common problems.

Supply Kit

Gift baskets may be a hobby or may be a profession for you, but in either case it's a skill you take very seriously. You might lead a PTA fund-raiser that calls for a hundred baskets and mugs to be auctioned during a black-tie charity event. As an office manager, perhaps you'll assist in creating fifty gift baskets for distribution to the most productive employees. Or you may be part of an awards committee and be called upon to make twenty-five gift baskets filled with donated items.

Whatever the case, the baskets must be transported from one location to another. Anything can and will happen between points A and B. Cellophane tears, balloons break, and ribbons tangle. You won't be ready for everything, but you can arm yourself against small problems.

How? Professional gift basket designers create what they call a supply kit that stays by their side in the workspace and travels with them by car to client destinations. This kit is a personal version of a doctor's bag and is as necessary to today's designers as eating and sleeping. It contains the basic supplies that turn a near disaster into success. A wire caddy coated in heavy white plastic is shown as an example. It includes:

- Scissors
- Wire cutters
- Glue dots
- Transparent tape
- One sheet of tissue paper
- One basket bag or 3 feet of cellophane
- Two handfuls of shred
- One spool of curling ribbon
- One star spray
- One additional enhancement

Designers also add foam, skewers, balloons, and accompanying supplies (cups and sticks) and extra bows. The exact contents of your kit will depend on what's important for your designs. Careful monitoring

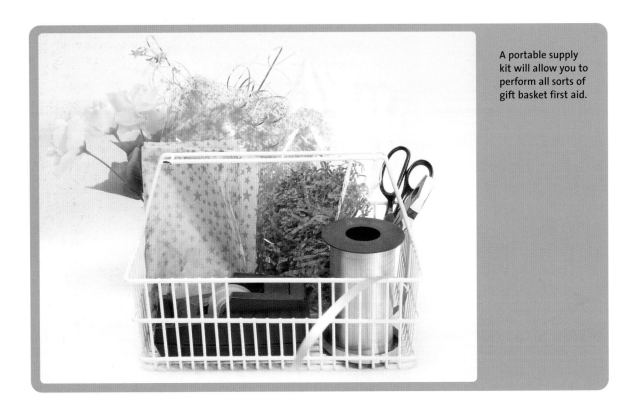

A portable supply kit will allow you to perform all sorts of gift basket first aid.

of the kit is also important. If the transparent tape expires and you forget to replenish it, the kit will be useless. The same is true for other supplies that you'll use up over time.

Each kit's contents will change periodically. A designer who's delivering a baby basket with yellow shred will replace the kit's green shred with yellow or may travel with several shred colors and check the kit before leaving. This kit is helpful on the road and also comes in handy if you design in one room but need a few supplies in another. Why pack yards of supplies when a few inches will do?

There's no need to buy a specific container to create a supply kit. A basket that's too old or unattractive is a good candidate. The same can be said for an old toolbox or another handled caddy. Shoe boxes and other cardboard containers don't work as well because they neither have a handle nor recover from bad weather.

Cellophane

Now that you've learned how to arm yourself for unexpected rips and tears, let's see how to put these tools to use. We'll start with cellophane problems.

Adding More on Top

Here are the supplies you'll need:

- Cellophane
- Curling ribbon
- Scissors

A tall fan of cellophane above the closing bow always raises the basket's perceived value. Cutting the wrong length or a sudden tear in the cello creates a stubby top that appears in disproportion to the

design. The solution isn't difficult to master, but you must exercise patience to fix this pesky problem.

Keep the short cello above the design together with curling ribbon, but remove the bow if tied in place. Cut a piece of curling ribbon approximately 2 feet long. Put it on the table, but keep it close to add around the design's neck. Cut a piece of cellophane across the roll and about 4 inches wide. Put the roll aside.

Using one hand, gather the entire cellophane together at the bottom of one end, leaving approximately $\frac{1}{2}$ inch below your hand. The cellophane above your hand resembles a fan topping.

Using both hands, place the gathered cellophane evenly around the short cello on the design. The new cellophane will encircle the short piece. Hold it in place, and tie the curling ribbon around the neck where the old and new cello meet. Place the curling ribbon below the ribbon, enclosing the old cello. This provides the new cello with extra support. Tie the bow around the new cellophane. Position the bow to cover the additional cello that hangs below the curling ribbon. If not, carefully snip the visible cellophane to shorten as needed.

If the new cello is uneven at the top, bring it together and cut it in a semicircle. Expand the cellophane on each side. The problem is solved.

TIP: Some designers add an extra fan topper onto their basket. This is done in the same way as described above. Instead of one cello color, two separate but coordinated toppers appear above the basket's neck. For example, if a basket is covered with plain cellophane, you can add printed cello around the plain wrap for a decorative topper.

1. Problem: Baskets need a tall fan of cellophane above the closing bow. This stubby top looks out of balance.

2. Solution: Cut an extra piece of cellophane and gather it in your hand.

3. Place the extra cellophane around the basket's short top.

4. Tie ribbon around the basket's neck where the old and new cello meet.

5. The ribbon effectively joins the two pieces of cello.

6. Add a bow to hide any extra cello.

7. Trim the cellophane evenly at the top.

8. Your fix is complete.

Patching Tears

You'll need these supplies:

- Cellophane
- Transparent tape
- Scissors

There are cellophane tears that can be patched and others that require the cello to be replaced. You will know which can be saved and which must be discarded according to the patch results.

Cellophane has a mind of its own. It usually doesn't tear unless pulled, pricked, or provoked—any or all of which are inevitable when you wrap a package. Problems can occur when inserting enhancements from the outside. For example, you add a pick or star spray by first deciding where the enhancement will rest, then placing a small piece of transparent tape where the enhancement will pierce the cello. Cut the cellophane with scissors by pinching the tape on the cellophane and making a small cut, then insert the enhancement through the cello and into the basket.

Transparent tape prevents the cellophane's tear from migrating. New designers, however, often forget to add tape or snip beyond the tape and onto the cello, which causes irreparable damage if not caught quickly.

The best way to repair a cellophane tear is by applying transparent tape, preferably on the cello's opposite side. This may require you to remove the bow, smooth the cellophane onto a flat surface, and tape as needed. Turn the taped cello toward the back of the design before reapplying it around the basket.

If the rip is in front and repairable, some designers add glue dots on top of the tape and press flower

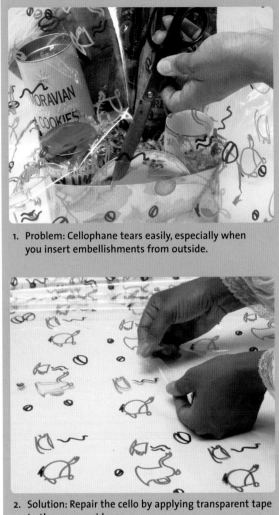

1. **Problem: Cellophane tears easily, especially when you insert embellishments from outside.**

2. **Solution: Repair the cello by applying transparent tape to the reverse side.**

petals or greenery on the dots. This solution isn't always workable, though; it depends on the location of the tear and its length. Still, try it before starting over.

TIP: If you replace the cellophane, store the old piece for use as a fan topper or as filler material within another basket or container.

Enhancements

When working with enhancements, you're likely to face two problems again and again: broken star spray and torn ribbons. Here are two solutions that might prove helpful.

Reviving Star Spray

You'll need:

- Basket or container design
- Star spray parts
- Scissors or skewer (optional)

You learned how to add star spray to a basket in chapter 5 (see page 41). Star spray consists of four parts:

- Multiple blades of onion grass
- Three wires decorated with stars
- One stem
- A center casing that holds it all together

This enhancement is purchased tall and straight, but the grass and wired stars are curled with scissors before basket insertion.

Pulling a blade of onion grass might cause it to break, but that's not a problem. There's always a piece of torn grass still wrapped in the casing. The end is curled, along with the remaining onion grass, and it's ready for placement. The three pieces of wired stars are curled around a pencil (for a thin curl), a marker (for a thick curl), or your finger. The wound curl is pulled upward to extend its height.

Pulling the wired stars may cause the piece to become dislodged. That's when your ingenuity tells you it's better to use the piece than throw it away. Remnants are easily added within baskets. Designers

1. Problem: Star spray can prove difficult. Pulling on the stars, for instance, may dislodge a piece.

2. Solution: If this happens, use spare pieces as embellishments in their own right.

place these renegade parts between products or wind them around handles. The stars and wire are brightly colored, creating a decorative appearance wherever they're added.

TIP: Wired stars are an attractive addition around the neck of a bottle or mug handle.

Lengthening a Bow's Ribbon

Here's what you'll need:

- Bow
- Curling ribbon
- Scissors

The expression "Haste makes waste" must have been coined by a person securing a bow on a basket. Rushing to finish a design usually results in a mini-disaster. Half the time it's stabilizing a product, and the other half it's a piece of curling ribbon breaking from a bow. This is not to say that ribbons break often, but when it happens, the situation is frustrating. One bright spot is that when the curling ribbon breaks, the bow is usually left undamaged and won't unravel to cause new problems.

Your solution is simple. Tying a piece of curling ribbon to the broken end is one option. However, the broken piece might be so short that it's impossible to do so. The better option is to thread a new strand of curling ribbon in the bow's midsection.

Use your scissors to cut the remaining strand of ribbon. Next, look at the bow to determine the best place to add the curling ribbon. It will be inserted between the loops. Thread the ribbon into place,

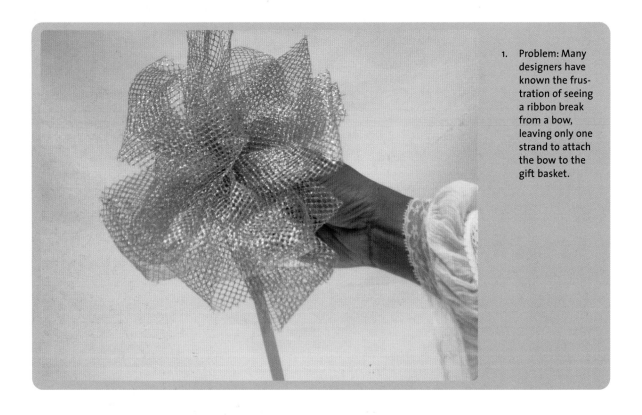

1. Problem: Many designers have known the frustration of seeing a ribbon break from a bow, leaving only one strand to attach the bow to the gift basket.

2. Solution: Cut the remaining ribbon with scissors.

3. Start over again by finding the bow's midsection.

4. Thread a new ribbon through the middle and bring both ends to the back.

5. The ribbon's insertion point should be masked by the bow's loops.

bringing the ends toward the back. If done correctly, the insertion point of the ribbon will be masked by the bow's loops. If not, look for a new insertion point and reinsert the ribbon.

Center the bow onto the basket, and tie the new curling ribbon strands around the neck. Curl the ends with scissors.

You'll encounter other snags while designing gift baskets. Most problems won't extend beyond the situations shown here, but by the time more advanced problems occur, you'll know how to turn a crisis into victory.

13

Designers and Their Gift Baskets

Regional Pros Share Their Inspirations

I travel from east to west to conduct seminars at industry shows and public events and meet no fewer than 1,000 gift basket designers each year. Some seminar attendees are just considering making gift baskets. Others have already started designing. Then there are the seasoned professionals who greet me as though I'm an old friend, whether or not we've met in the past.

Designers at every stage of the craft constantly teach me something new. Their spirit and enthusiasm tell me that gift baskets aren't just products; they are a way of life that individuals proudly embrace as their everyday work. It's the love of the craft that keeps us all designing.

The four designers you're about to meet embody the creative spirit that gift basket makers share around the world. Let me introduce you to these regional pros, and let's take a close look at some of their most successful basket designs to date.

Flora Morris Brown, Ph.D.:
Gift Basket Business World
Anaheim, California

On a typical trip to Southern California, I expect three things: (1) the sun, (2) traffic congestion, and (3) two incredibly styled gift baskets waiting for my arrival. Flora is the designing diva that I aspire to become. I pause to admire her work, then she introduces me to her masterpieces: Relaxation Time and the California Garden.

Flora names her baskets because it gives each a personality, and that's what her clients love. Realtors are especially fond of these designs, which they buy in bulk for their homeowners and sellers to thank them for their business. After fifteen years of designing, Flora has tapped into Realtors' referral markets, and that means lots of repeat customers. It's one reason why this award-winning designer's business continues to thrive. Flora is gifted with a visual imagination, which allows her to create a gift basket in her mind before she starts working with her hands. She made the Relaxation Time for Realtors who prefer out-of-the-ordinary baskets. It includes a bath pillow, bath gloves, bath gel, bath fizz balls, body brushes, pumice stone, reflexology socks, hair turban, and bath lotion, all arranged in a large oval tin finished with gold-colored trim.

The bath gloves drape downward over the tin's rim, a clever technique that allows the gloves to be showcased rather than hidden elsewhere. A gel eye mask, head wrap, and relaxation CD let the homeowner slip into much-needed quiet time after hectic moving tasks. An iridescent bow and clear ornament picks that resemble bubbles add to the recipient's anticipation of rejuvenation.

Flora Morris Brown's Relaxation Time basket.

Under this relaxation bundle are layers of newsprint and shred, but there's less support on top. Flora has mastered a design style that eliminated the need for glue dots and tape. That keeps her design time to a minimum and lets the receiver take the gift apart faster. She does, however, encourage beginners to "take advantage of glue dots and tape as needed." The finished product is shrink-wrapped so that the products stay securely in place.

Flora loves to use enhancements. She says it's the "key to bringing the basket alive. Adding enhancements and a bow will separate you from an amateur."

Flora's California Garden basket combines useful garden products—including spades and a bird house—in a surprising base.

This design comes alive with the addition of moss, pine, and floral embellishments.

She suggests buying quality products that look real and using these items sparingly. Most of her enhancements are purchased after the holidays when deep discounts prevail.

Another of Flora's top sellers is the California Garden basket. It's one of her "wild baskets" because "it's so creative and wows people." A water hose acts as the foundation. It's exactly as it was when initially purchased, wound together and secured with plastic ties.

The inner cavity is filled with newsprint and shred. A birdhouse is positioned on top and gently pushed downward so it doesn't wobble. Recipients are elated with the shovels added on each side, sunblock, garden book, Bath Buddies soap with butterfly, hummingbird nectar (bird food), plant seeds, and hand sanitizer. This design is wrapped twice before delivery, with shrink wrap on the inside and cellophane on the outside. The double coating stabilizes the package and provides a soft outer covering.

Flora suggests that you "bring your designs alive with something living." As an example, she glued a faux bird to the top of the house and added moss and pine embellishments that don't resemble Christmas decorations.

After many years of successfully running her own gift basket business, Flora created www.giftbasket businessworld.com, where she helps new and veteran designers and gift retailers with tips and resource materials. Her classes, private consultations, training DVDs, information-packed audio CDs, and free weekly newsletter help many others create profitable gift basket businesses of their own.

Dana Sonia:
Gift Baskets by Your Design
Chichester, New Hampshire

The moment Dana said "Hello" on the phone told me I was about to take a fantastic voyage with a designer who's passionate and energetic about her role in the gift basket industry. As we spoke, it was easy to understand why clients choose her for their extraordinary baskets and how her dedication to detail makes Dana New Hampshire's rising star.

"I heard a statistic that says only one in ten people is happy in their job, and I'm one of the lucky ones," Dana told me. She generously shared her thoughts on the triumphs and challenges of running a business from a third-floor studio within her home.

"We specialize in New Hampshire baskets, but it hasn't limited us," says Dana. "We're not just rustic up here, we're also high-end. We change the image of what New Hampshire has to offer." One gift basket, named for the state's Balsams Grand Resort Hotel, is priced at $250, "and it sells," says Dana. She's found success in naming each of her state-themed baskets. "People like things to be named. It gives the baskets more personality."

There's another reason why New Hampshire baskets are her specialty. Dana is committed to supporting the local economy. "It works out really well," she says, and wholesalers reciprocate in kind, referring business her way.

The featured gift basket sparkles with New Hampshire appeal. It begins with a large, round basket filled with packing paper and topped with cream-colored shred. The contents include pancake mix, syrup, chutney, dips, pear-spice bread mix, flavored oil, chocolates, and teas. Floral vines, flowers, and a large bow provide visual elegance.

Sales have increased each year, an outcome that Dana didn't think about when she first opened, especially because of the timing. "I requested my business license on September 9, 2001, and took my first order on September 10." A day later tragedy struck in New York, Washington, and Pennsylvania, but Dana was determined to succeed. "It really didn't make me think I couldn't do this business. I felt more passionate to start."

Dana originally grew up in south Florida. She moved to New Hampshire in 1997 and worked for a government information center providing help to people needing passports. The eight years she spent there had its ups and downs. "The company said they didn't want me to focus on customer service. They told me that I was helping people too much. I realized that if I couldn't help people, I couldn't do my job. I left there in May 2001 and started my business in September."

For three months Dana focused on new opportunities. Her husband, a detective with the state's major crime unit, encouraged her to consider every angle before deciding. "I wanted a business, not a hobby. I knew I wanted to work for myself." She found ideas on the Small Business Administration's Web site, but then fate intervened. While looking through *Yankee Magazine*, Dana found herself designing a gift basket on a stray envelope as she leafed through the pages. "I had never done it (made a basket) before." She began researching gift baskets on the Web and decided that making customized gifts was her calling.

In the early 1990s, there was little information on

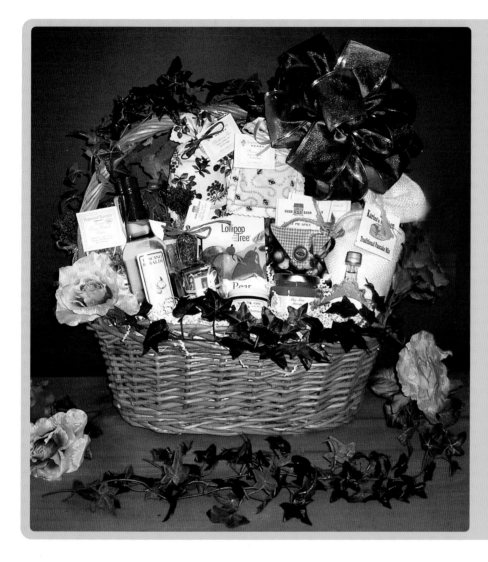

the Internet about making gift baskets. By the time Dana started her research, there was an abundance of details provided on industry sites. "You get overwhelmed," she says. Dana paced herself while learning, which included reading opinions on gift basket message boards. She invested in her future by attending a gift basket convention. Being around experts and aspiring designers allowed her to focus on how to proceed. She decided to have a targeted business approach, which led to New Hampshire–themed baskets. "I took information from the conference to decide which way I wanted to grow."

As Dana started selecting basket themes, she quickly learned that the best choices depend on client preferences. "I started the business thinking I'm not going to do this basket and that basket," she explains. "You soon realize you don't do what you like; you do what your customers like." One specialty gift Dana recently created was an Oreos basket. "The client's father was having surgery, and we made it for him using a cool red bucket filled with two packs, double stuffed, and other varieties."

Pricing her baskets was another challenge. "I realized that I was pricing baskets according to what I would spend. I had to think outside of that barrier." This boils down to not overpricing the client, but rather being consistent and charging them a reasonable price. During the order process, Dana prefers to speak directly with customers to make sure their request is completely understood. "Communication is so important. I have to ask, or I'm going to get it wrong." One example of this is when she spoke with a client by phone rather than by e-mail, the traditional way they communicate. He "ordered a $150 basket for a secretary and later told me that he wanted something 'slightly bigger' for another person. Had I assumed what 'slightly bigger' meant, I would have made a $175 basket when what he wanted was a $250 basket. I wouldn't have met the needs of my customer or his recipient."

Dana's list has grown to more than 400 clients, including California Governor Arnold Schwarzenegger. To date, she has shipped baskets throughout the United States and to eight other countries. There was a time when Dana would stress over not getting every sale. "Now I don't worry about the ones that got away." She remembers the name of everyone who orders, maintains a profile of each client, and keeps a log of every order. Her four children, ages two to fifteen, lend a hand when needed, whether to complete designs or make deliveries. Friends and family members also help Dana during busy times. While the third floor of her home is the design center, the basement is the shipping area, and the two-car garage is available to store mega-orders. Her home includes six acres of land, and Dana's sights are set on building a facility on the property to streamline the business.

Marketing is a constant challenge for gift basket designers; however, Dana's business has grown organically. "It's all word of mouth, so imagine what I can do if I market." This method is not for everyone, and Dana cautions new designers against believing marketing isn't a necessity. "Good marketing materials are not to be overlooked. They are very important." Dana's business card features one of her signature baskets. The card's background color is a warm green, and the card is vertically positioned. "People see what you can do right away through the card."

Mixing business with charity comes naturally to Dana. "We're very involved with the Make a Wish Foundation. We donate gifts to go with the wishes. Each gift is based on the likes, dislikes, and illnesses of the children. It's been great because we want to touch their lives." She also creates sports-themed baskets, and one of her baskets raised $5,000 for charity.

Dana shares her wisdom with as much passion and energy as she puts in her business: "Stay true to yourself and your goals. If I can start a business two days before a tragedy and become successful, anything is possible."

Elaine Essary:

The Basket Bar, Manhattan, Illinois

One look at Elaine and I could see a dynamo in the making. With just a few years of business under her belt, the fire in her eyes still flickers with determination to make her mark. Elaine started her business in December 2001. She had worked as a recruitment manager/corporate trainer but was laid off due to downsizing after the 9/11 tragedies. Elaine began making gift baskets for family and friends. "People loved them," she says, and that gave her the inspiration to consider a new career.

Elaine was determined to start with as much knowledge as possible, so she invested three months in research, reading books on what it's like to become a designer. She also purchased general business books. "I put lots of dollars into it." Elaine visited gift basket message boards on the Internet for ideas and insight. She soon registered her business name and began attending trade shows to buy products at wholesale cost. The purchases are stored in her basement, which she converted into a design studio. But the trade-off has been a business that offers impressive rewards.

The featured holiday basket, created in a gold sleigh, contains enough goods for an entire group to enjoy. Packing paper cushions the bottom before a layer of white and gold-mixed shred is added. When choosing products, Elaine buys a variety of items with varying heights to create a well-rounded design. This gift includes rum cake, chocolates, gingerbread cookies, snack mix, mulling spices, toffee, white- and milk-chocolate-drizzled pretzels, popcorn, fudge cookies, and coffee. She uses skewers and glue dots to anchor

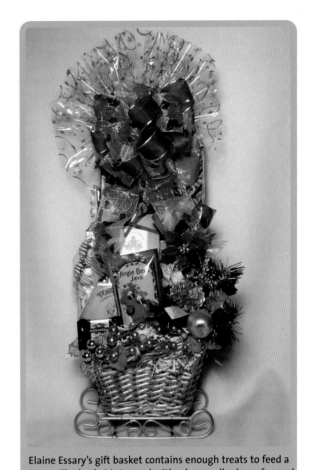

Elaine Essary's gift basket contains enough treats to feed a group. The basket is topped with a large cellophane fan and a wired bow.

her products. You may be tempted to make a meal of these goodies, but when you're in business, that is not a good idea. "It's money," says Elaine, "so I don't even think about eating it."

The cost of picks and flowers adds up, and Elaine prefers to spend money on foods and snacks. Two basket products requested most often are white-chocolate popcorn and chocolate-covered graham

Elaine anchors the tallest products with skewers and glue dots.

crackers. Items made in Illinois top Elaine's must-have list, because she has easy access to manufacturers when she needs to fill an order quickly. But quickness is balanced with a double-check of expiration dates. Elaine monitors all products for freshness to ensure that nothing stale is mistakenly added.

The cellophane fan behind the large bow is made with a Bowdabra machine and then tied to a tall plastic stick. Elaine ties it on with curling ribbon before pairing it with the bow for added enhancement. She chooses cellophane to cover her designs rather than shrink wrap.

Eighty-five percent of her sales are to corporate customers, some of which are pharmaceutical companies that Elaine finds through networking. Other sales are Internet orders placed by customers who visit her Web site. Elaine's bank is also a client. She combined the bank's imprinted mug with coffee and biscotti and also imprinted its name on ribbon using a machine. She walked in and presented the bank's president with the mug. The two began talking, and Elaine learned that the president planned to send gifts and needed to satisfy a large volume of donation requests for gift baskets. This interaction netted the account for Elaine.

Not being content to rest on her laurels, Elaine joined several organizations, including multiple chambers of commerce and a home-builders association. Elaine doesn't fear talking about her business to new people. Her motto is, "The worst they can say is no."

Savvy designers know how to recruit free help. Elaine found her marketing intern at a local college. He helps her develop marketing plans, which earns him college credits. It's a great arrangement for both parties. She also urges anyone who is developing a business Web site to work with someone who not only knows the technical end but is savvy when it comes to optimization. "A Web site doesn't sell itself just because it's on the Web. There is a lot of competition these days, and you need to help people find you easily."

Elaine urges anyone who wants to make gift baskets to "do your homework." It will help limit mistakes and keep the fire in your eyes burning for years.

Lise Schleicher:

BasketWorks, Northbrook, Illinois

There are two choices after ten years in business: You sink or you swim. Where does Lise Schleicher stand? Let's just say she's a mermaid with a buoyant personality to match.

Lise opened her gift basket business in 1997 after searching for a career that matched her skills. She worked in retail for two years and a floral shop for four years. That's where she learned to make bows and much more. Color matching was another requirement. Today all this knowledge helps her make smart inventory choices. For example, she prefers natural-colored baskets, which she sprays white for baby baskets and gold or silver for holiday gifts. Prepainted baskets offer Lise less versatility. "You can do many things and create unique themes using the color white as the backdrop," she explains.

It's no wonder that her featured basket is white and black. Packing peanuts are added inside this tuxedo container. The peanuts are placed in tissue paper and rolled for stabilization. Smoked salmon pâté, chocolate-covered pretzels, cookies, and other confections are matched up. Lise adds unique embellishments in her baskets such as Mylar poufs and colored or patterned napkins. Here, the platinum-colored bow and matching fabric are all that's needed to create an elegant image.

Lise Schleicher transformed a slow-moving millennium container into her popular Puttin' on the Ritz basket. The platinum-colored fabric and bow create a clean, sophisticated look.

This design won an award at a gift basket convention, but it wasn't always a winner. Lise purchased these containers for the millennium, but they didn't sell. She would have been stuck with unmovable inventory had she not considered an alternative use. Lise searched for ribbon and fabric that would transform the container and called the design Puttin' on the Ritz. The new image generated hefty sales. It sells not only for everyday occasions but also for weddings, anniversaries, thank-you gifts, and to corporations that love it because they like the design's "clean look."

Lise's biggest customers are home builders, mortgage brokers, a machinery firm, a concierge firm, Chicago's United Center, the University of Chicago Celiac Disease Program, and Broadway in Chicago (formerly The Schubert Theater). The latter orders gift baskets for VIPs, headliners, and supporters. Lise enjoys serving clients in different industries, describing it as "being all over the map." The variety keeps her designs fresh and innovative.

Some clients request ad specialty items, such as mugs, in their baskets. That's the reason Lise maintains a broad inventory, which includes many containers. Client favorites include Thank-You and Get Well baskets. A ribbon imprinter is invaluable in providing custom ribbon in a flash.

Containers are important, but Lise estimates that 75 percent of her sales are baskets, especially for new babies. Approximately 50 percent of sales are food baskets that incorporate themed cookies, chocolate chip cookies, snack mixes, kosher items,

tortilla chips, dipping pretzels and mustards, tea, mulling cider, dips, and crackers. Small gift books, coffee, jelly beans, and white-chocolate bark are some of the more popular inventory.

Lise creates dozens of new designs a year, and everything is a custom creation. One item will strike her, and that's when the idea for a whole package begins. Last year copper ribbon was high on Lise's list. This year silk flowers are the target. "I find something—coffee, flowers—and it sets me off. We're also doing lots this year with Mylar balloons and sheer organza."

Lise has a bachelor's degree in business management and a master's in labor relations. Her sister, Caren, is the marketing guru who helps Lise develop products and services that spread the word about her business. This includes making calls to potential customers and assisting Lise at expos and open-house events. Lise and Caren also mail specially printed postcards to prospects and customers. The Internet plays a major role in marketing. "We're now relying more on a well-optimized Web site and publishing online newsletters."

Because of her business background, Lise knew that she had to start networking to sell her designs, so she joined a networking group three months after opening for business. She's now a member of two chambers of commerce and a networking group.

Lise sums up why swimming to success is her only option: "I'm a business person first, creative person second, and it all balances out."

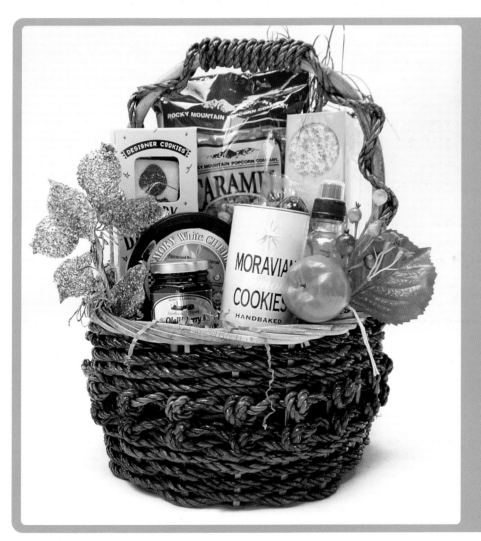

The traditional all-occasion gift basket, ready to be customized for a woman or a man.

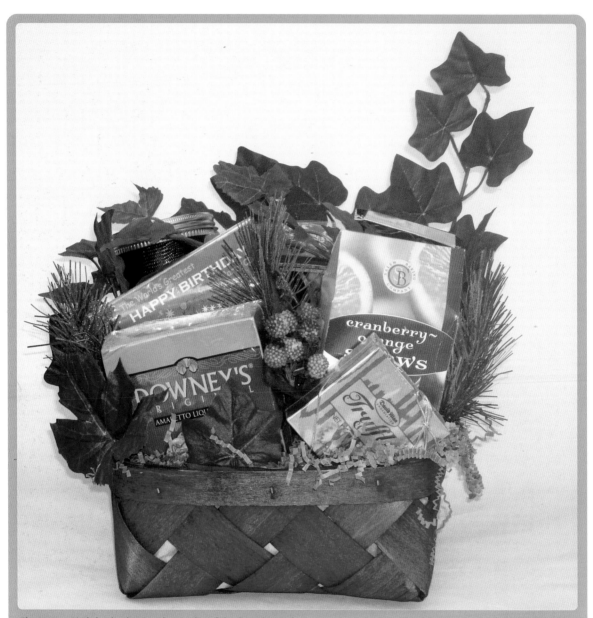

The Happy Birthday basket employs a cheerful color scheme for a man or woman.

A purple-and-white color scheme gives the Congratulations basket an elegant look.

Even this tiny Thank-you basket makes a big impression on the recipient.

Sparkling cider in a wine basket along with a wineglass and a few snacks make up the Good Luck basket.

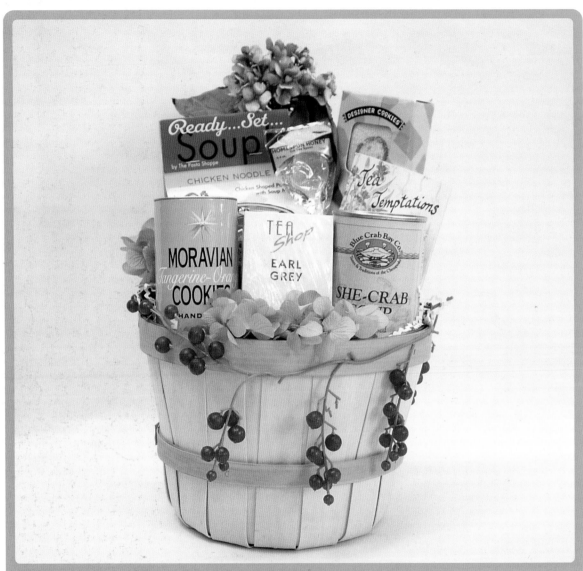

The Get-Well basket is a fruit basket full of soothing soups and teas.

Luxurious bath products are included in the Spa basket. A bath pillow and slippers complete this design.

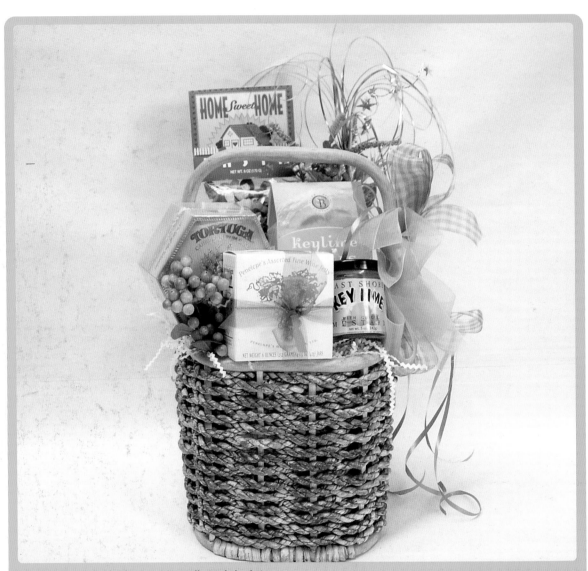

The Housewarming basket is set in a tall, sturdy basket.

Orange gingham and yellow organza accentuate a Housewarming basket, whose contents are both functional and fun.

The Baby basket can be large . . .

. . . or small, and for either a girl or a boy, by changing containers and the number of products included.

A burgundy-colored table runner adds warmth and contrast to the whites of this Wedding basket. Scones, jams, chocolates, and candles are arranged in a picnic basket for the newlyweds.

A Bereavement basket needn't be large to extend condolences and comfort. Red, white, and green make a tasteful color scheme.

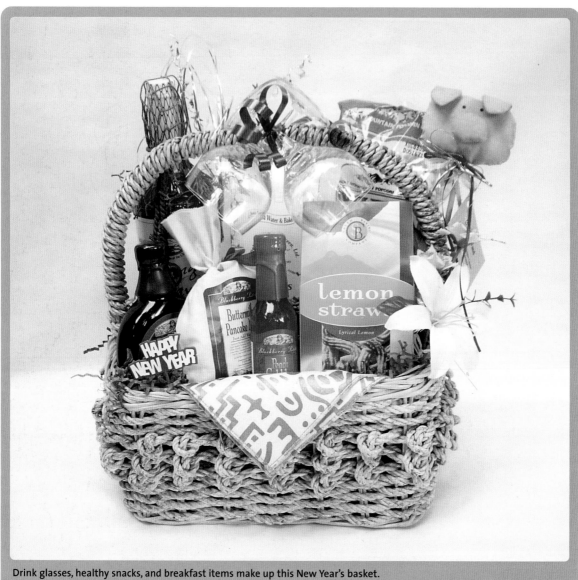

Drink glasses, healthy snacks, and breakfast items make up this New Year's basket.

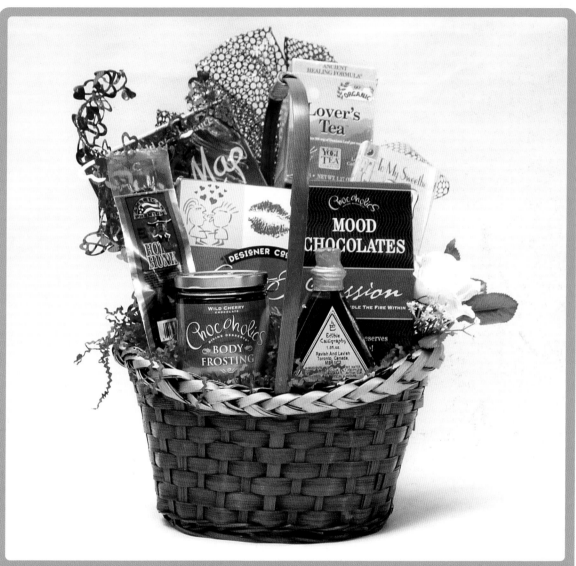

Designed in the colors of the day, this Valentine's basket is embellished with a heart spray, flowers, a homemade bow, and punchinello ribbon.

What mother doesn't need a little help? That's where this wheelbarrow-shaped Mother's Day basket comes in, filled with products chosen especially for Mom.

The Father's Day basket is a study in open-and-eat snacks.

Star spray, a campaign hat, and red shred liven up this July 4th design.

The Thanksgiving box is made more colorful and festive by adding coordinating tissue and enhancements.

Christmas is far and away the biggest gift-basket-giving day of the year. This Christmas basket is designed to be appropriate for a man or a woman.

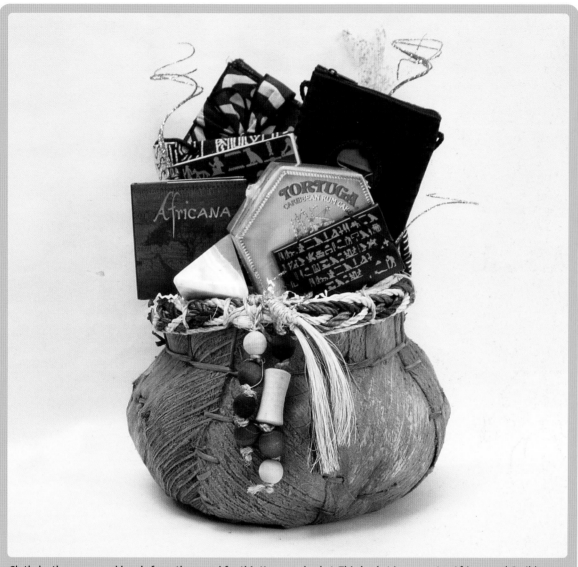

Cloth, leather, rope, and beads form the vessel for this Kwanzaa basket. This basket incorporates African- and Caribbean-based products and colors.

The Fruit-Decorated box uses a beautiful, reusable container.

This colorful box says "thank-you" in many different languages.

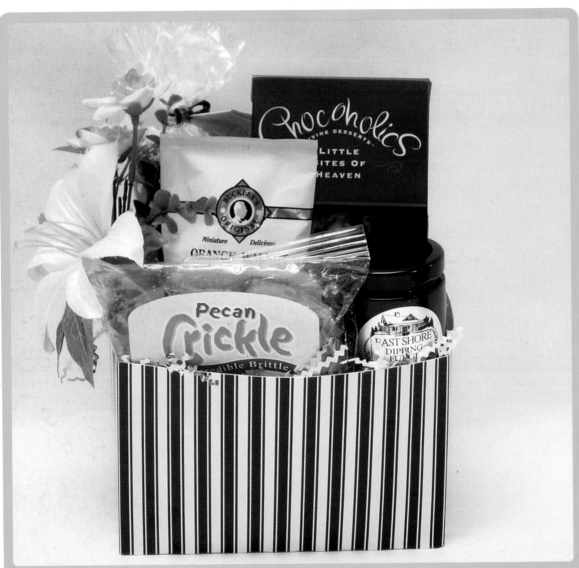

The Black-and-White-Striped box makes a classic, elegant corporate or congratulatory gift. Use shred to add color.

A white brocade hat box, pink picks, and pink shred complete the Chocoholic design.

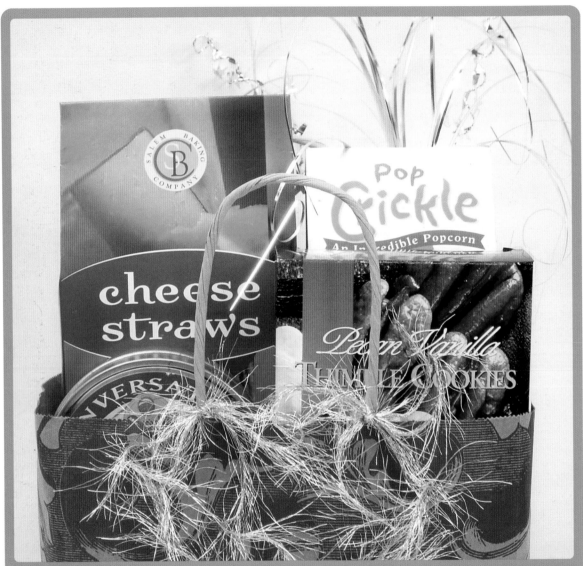

A burgundy fleur-de-lis patterned bag, silver eyelash ribbon, and metallic star spray form the Tote bag.

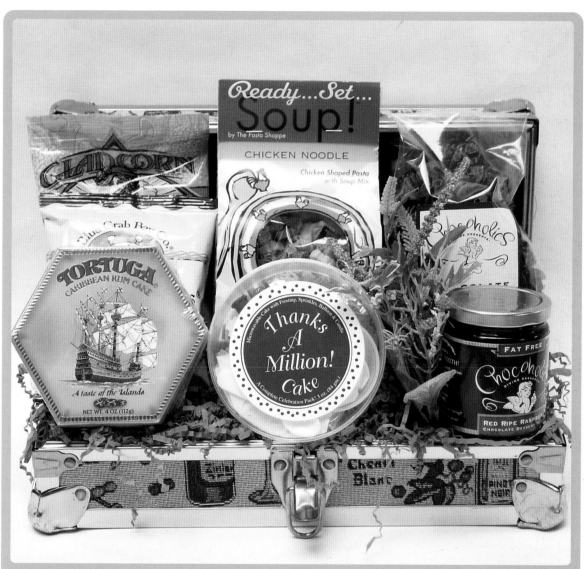

A trunk makes a popular gift container. Here the theme is Thanks a Million, but you can be as creative as you like. Yard sales make a good source for trunks.

An upside-down box serves as the base for this vertical Gourmet Tower of treats.

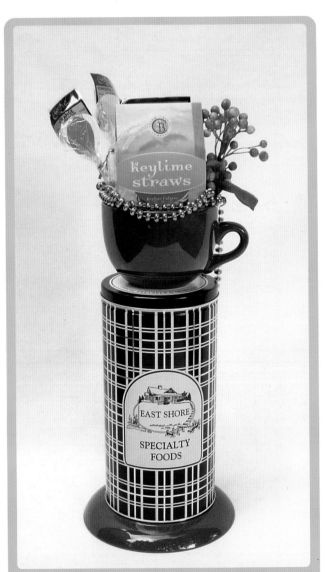

The Latte Tower combines snacks and beverages with a cup and saucer.

Mugs make charming gift receptacles. You might choose one that's personalized (left) or frosted (right). Glue dots between the products hold everything securely.

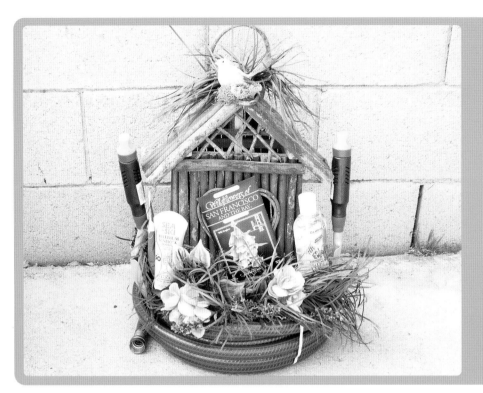

Award-winning designer Flora Morris Brown has created the California Garden basket, which is a big hit with homeowners. A water hose serves as its base.

Flora Morris Brown's Relaxation Time basket will pamper recipients.

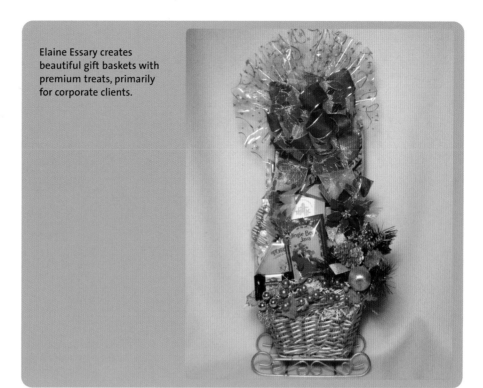

Elaine Essary creates beautiful gift baskets with premium treats, primarily for corporate clients.

Lise Schleicher created her award-winning Puttin' on the Ritz basket by combining a tuxedo container, smoked salmon pâté, and a platinum-colored bow.

Dana Sonia designed this bountiful gift basket, which is enhanced with a large bow for visual elegance.

Appendix

Apex Gift Foods

2815 Penn Avenue

Pittsburgh, PA 15222

(412) 261-4242 or (800) 348-2369

Fax: (800) 315-2739

www.apexgiftfoods.com

Over 300 shelf-stable gourmet treats and a complete line of packaging supplies and unique trimmings. Personal, professional customer service. Prompt shipping. Free full-color catalog available, plus special Web site promotions and blog.

Baskets, Containers, & More

P.O. Box 7547

Akron, OH 44306

(800) 773-2554

Fax: (800) 773-3575

www.directfloral.com

A wholesale floral-supplies company that offers a wide variety of high-quality baskets, containers, and gift basket supplies. No minimum order requirement, and same-day shipping.

Brownlow Gifts

6309 Airport Freeway

Fort Worth, TX 76117

(817) 831-3831 or (800) 433-7610

Fax: (817) 831-7025

www.brownlowgift.com

Brownlow Gifts produces themed collections including stationery, ceramic, resin, and gourmet gifts, many with suggested retail prices of $10 or less. Scripture versions of most products are also available.

Creative Gift Packaging Inc.

4722 Ellenboro Road

Mooresboro, NC 28114

(704) 434-8404 or (866) 443-8706

Fax: (704) 434-8457

www.cgpackaging.com or www.creativegift packaging.com

One-stop shopping for all your gift basket supplies including cellophane, shred, bows, ribbons, Boxco boxes, and gourmet foods. No minimum order requirement.

David Alan Chocolatier

1700 North Lebanon Street

P.O. Box 588

Lebanon, IN 46052

(800) 428-2310

www.davidalanchocolatier.com

Swiss-style chocolate truffles. Their small boxes are ideal for gift baskets. Low minimum.

Dobson Products

P.O. Box 496027

Chicago, IL 60649

(773) 734-5325 or (800) 358-7626

Fax: (773) 734-3817

www.dobsonproducts.com

The single source for unique Afrocentric and Greek fraternity, sorority, and Masonic gift items. Mouse pads, light-switch covers, coffee mugs, and desk accessories are available.

Eldorado

2325 West Midway Boulevard

Broomfield, CO 80020

(303) 444-4622 or (800) 525-0848

Fax: (303) 444-0696

www.eldoradoparty.com

Major wholesaler and distributor of romantic and intimate gift selections for wedding, honeymoon, anniversary, birthday, holiday, bachelorette, and other fun party supplies, plus edibles, fantasy wear, and so much more!

Gift Basket Business

P.O. Box 31, River Street Station

Paterson, NJ 07544-0031

(973) 279-2799

www.giftbasketbusiness.com

A complete source for educational materials, including books, DVDs, product sources, a free newsletter, online tips and articles, a blog, and more to make gift baskets for fun or profit.

Gift Basket Business World

446 South Anaheim Hills Road

Anaheim, CA 92807

(714) 637-1455

www.giftbasketbusinessworld.com

Informative booklets, free newsletter, tip sheets, and other lucrative resources for gift basket businesses on the grow.

Gift Basket Tutorials

www.giftbaskettutorials.com

Online instructional videos offering gift basket tips and techniques for beginning and advanced designers.

Highland Beef Farms

P.O. Box 2414

Reston, VA 20195

(800) 869-6320

Fax: (800) 454-5032

www.highlandbeeffarms.com

Top-quality meat, turkey, and cheese snacks. Featuring the "Nutrition on the Run" product line for the health-conscious consumer.

Karen's Keepsakes, LLC
11 Anthony Avenue
Edison, NJ 08820
(908) 753-5756 or (800) 231-9137
Fax: (908) 561-3702
www.karenskeepsakes.com/gb
Baby footprint and handprint kits, Radio Flyer® wagons, baby scrubs, plush toys, banks, frames, CDs for babies and adults, microwave cakes, gourmet foods, paw-print kits, pet treats, and adult products.

Maine Line Products, Inc.
P.O. Box 130
Greenwood, ME 04255
(207) 875-2522 or (800) 874-0484
Fax: (207) 875-2992
www.mainelineproducts.com
Manufactures approximately fifty-five sizes of wooden crates and boxes. Most are priced between $1 and $3.

Music For Baskets
1724 Westgate Road
Eau Claire, WI 54703
(715) 836-9800 or (800) 233-6356
Fax: (715) 836-9733
www.musicforbaskets.com
Music For Baskets offers a wonderful selection of CDs with cover art and music created to complement gift basket themes and colors. Incomparable products and customer service. See and hear the CDs online, then buy online or by phone.

Nashville Wraps
242 Molly Walton Drive
Hendersonville, TN 37075
(800) 547-9727
Fax: (800) 646-0046
www.nashvillewraps.com
Large selection of gift and gourmet packaging—bags, boxes, ribbon, tissue, and related packaging products. Exquisite product design, competitive prices, and a high degree of service.

Pendergrass Inc.
115 North Main Street
Chaffee, MO 63740
(573) 887-4144 or (800) 748-7655
Fax: (573) 887-6086
www.pendergrassinc.com
Full line of bath, body, and spa accessories for women, men, and children. Spa gift sets also available for all categories. Contact Pendergrass to obtain the wholesale password.

Quality Components Unlimited, Inc.
6240-2 Metro Plantation Road
Fort Myers, FL 33966
(800) 729-2205
Fax: (239) 332-2205
www.qcu.com
The only full-service, one-stop source for the gift basket industry. Gourmet foods, unique baskets and containers, shrink wrap, baby products, ribbons, and more!

Roof Basket Works, Inc.
1514 Pisgah Church Road
Lexington, SC 29072
(803) 359-6808 or (800) 368-8425
Fax: (803) 359-5661
www.roofbasket.com
Handmade, inexpensive wooden baskets in a variety
of colors and styles. Easy for you to customize into any
theme. No minimum order requirement.

Stephan Baby
3 Pequignot Drive
Pierceton, IN 46562
(574) 594-2131 or (800) 359-2917
Fax: (574) 594-2215
www.stephanbaby.net
Heartwarming baby gifts that are uniquely designed
and moderately priced. Choose from plush toys, silver-
plated gift sets, photo books and frames, infant clothing, and accessories.

The Ya-Hoo! Baking Co.
5302 Texoma Parkway
Sherman, TX 75090
(903) 893-8151 or (800) 575-9373
Fax: (903) 893-5036
www.cakesforbaskets.com
The Ya-Hoo! Baking Co. has been baking high-quality
bakery food gifts since 1944. They offer a unique group
of shelf-stable cakes packaged especially for baskets.
Each cake is moist and delicious and will stay fresh for
nine to twenty-four months, depending on type.

About the Author

Shirley George Frazier is president and founder of Sweet Survival, a retail consulting firm specializing in gift basket design, marketing, and business development. Recognized internationally as an industry expert, Shirley works with home-based designers, retail-shop owners, florists, and department-store managers to create and launch plans to increase profits on and off the Web. She is the author of *How to Start a Home-Based Gift Basket Business* and *Marketing Strategies for the Home-Based Business: Solutions You Can Use Today*, published by The Globe Pequot Press. Shirley also writes articles for and is quoted in numerous publications. She travels extensively to speak on gift-industry and business topics and appears on television as an industry spokesperson. Shirley lives in Paterson, New Jersey, with her husband, John; daughter, Genesis; and dogs, Pepper and Daisy.

Have You Ever Dreamed of Starting Your Own
Gift Basket Business?

Have you been hesitant to put your plans into action?

How to Start a Home-Based Gift Basket Business contains all the necessary tools and success strategies you will need to launch and grow your own business!

Successful home-based gift basket entrepreneur Shirley George Frazier will show you how to cultivate your creativity and employ savvy marketing techniques to run a thriving gift basket business.

From painless record keeping to savvy marketing techniques her step-by-step methods are realistic, innovative, and easy to understand.

Includes information on how to:

◆ develop a business plan,

◆ estimate your start-up costs,

◆ price your services,

◆ stay profitable once you're in business,

◆ develop a web site and generate traffic to your site,

and much more!

How to Start a Home-Based Gift Basket Business, 4th edition

$18.95 · paperback · 33 b&w illustrations, 31 charts and checklists

Available now from your favorite bookseller or visit www.GlobePequot.com or call (800) 243-0495